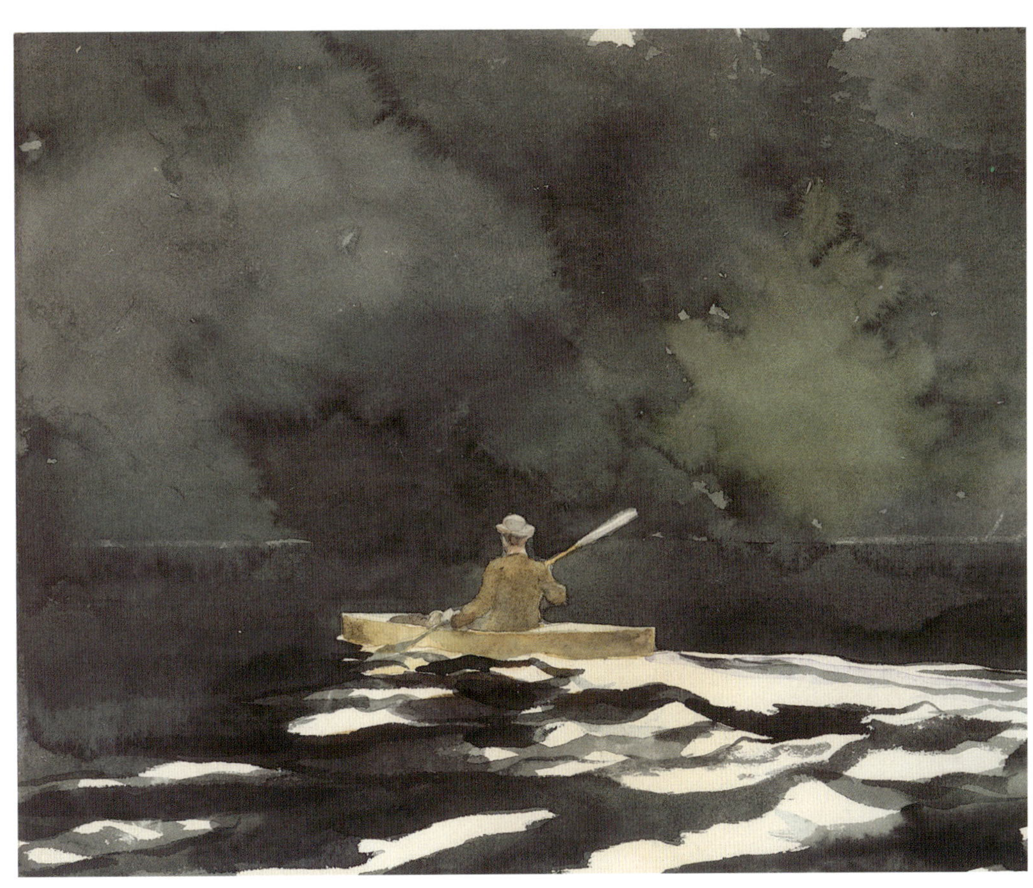

Above and front cover: Winslow Homer, *Paddling at Dusk*, 1892.

Voices in the gallery:

Grant Holcomb, Editor

The University of Rochester Press Ⓡ

writers on art

Front cover and frontispiece: Winslow Homer, *Paddling at Dusk*, 1892, p. 62.

Back cover: Jacob Lawrence, *Summer Street Scene in Harlem*, 1948, p. 64.

The University of Rochester Press is an imprint of Boydell & Brewer, Inc.

668 Mt. Hope Avenue, Rochester, NY 14620, USA;

and of Boydell & Brewer, Ltd.

P.O. Box 9, Woodbridge, Suffolk IP12 3DF, UK.

Library of Congress Cataloging-in-Publication Data

Voices in the gallery: writers on art / [editor, Grant Holcomb].

     p. cm.

   "Original essays and poetry on works of art from the Memorial Art Gallery, Rochester, New York."

   ISBN 1-58046-092-5

   1. Art–Poetry. 2. American poetry–20th century. 3. University of Rochester. Memorial Art Gallery–Poetry. 4. University of Rochester. Memorial Art Gallery. 5. Art. I. Holcomb, Grant. II. University of Rochester. Memorial Art Gallery.

PS595.A75 V65 2001

810.8'0357–dc21

                        2001033175

Acknowledgments

To acknowledge the forty writers who participated in this venture is both an honor and a privilege. They have been enthusiastic, supportive and gracious from the very beginning. Robert Creeley was the first to respond and I was delighted when he selected Vuillard's *Portrait of Lugné Poë* as it conveys, through color, form and composition, the concentration, dedication and imagination of the writer. To the poets and novelists go first thanks.

The Estate of David Cohen provided the initial funding for this project and, in turn, it was furthered by the generous support of long-time Gallery friend Dorothee Schwartz. I trust that this publication properly honors the memory of both David Cohen and Dorothee Schwartz.

I remain deeply grateful for the support given by the New York State Council on the Arts and, in particular, Kristin Herron, Director of the Museum Program, who encouraged the project from the beginning. A grant from the Institute of Museum and Library Science provided necessary funding for photography. Additional support was provided by the Thomas H. and Marion Hawks Fund.

My assistant, Carolyn Buechel Wilson, provided much-needed technical and organizational assistance throughout. She has prodded and guided, corrected and counseled. For this,

Grant Holcomb

(2001)

and more, I am most thankful. Chris Garland, the Gallery's Assistant Director of Development, was instrumental in developing funding proposals that enabled us, in the end, to publish this book. Deborah Rothman, the Gallery's Director of Public Relations and Marketing, was our chief liaison with the University of Rochester Press and was instrumental in seeing the publication through to completion. Marjorie Searl (Chief Curator), Marlene Hamann-Whitmore (Assistant Curator of Education), Nancy Norwood (Curator of European Art), Monica Simpson (Registrar), Lu Harper (Librarian), along with Kathy Ertsgaard, Chrisa Katsampes and Susan Nurse, answered all questions regarding artists, works of art, photographs in the collection and even location of specific landscape sites. Kim Hallatt, our chief financial officer, provided keen financial oversight, while the support and enthusiasm of Susan Dodge Peters, Director of Education, will result in a similar project designed for students in the Rochester area. Together, they well represent a dedicated and most able staff.

The support and good counsel of Brian Thompson, Provost Emeritus at the University of Rochester and Chairman of the Editorial Board of the University of Rochester Press, Susan Dykstra-Poel, Managing Director of the Press, and Tim Madigan, Editorial Director, were also helpful, indeed, instrumental in realizing the publication. Their encouragement, courtesy and friendship are appreciated.

Leslie Van Auken, of Van Auken Margolis & Associates, designed the book. Her professional skills and talents are obvious and her good suggestions throughout the process of publication appreciated. Wayne Scheible, of Flower City Printing, has been exceedingly generous to the Gallery. We remain indebted to him, and to Dan Georger, for their work and kind support. Our thanks also to Tucker Printers for bringing this project to a successful conclusion.

Conversations and correspondence with writers Bill Heyen, Jerry Ramsey, Joanna Scott, Jim Longenbach, Richard Tillinghast and Ed Hirsch, as well as with Joe Flaherty of Writers & Books, Inc. and Steve Huff and Thom Ward at BOA Editions, enhanced, enriched and sustained the effort. John and Pam Blanpied also provided keen commentary and invaluable advice as copy editors.

Finally, thanks to my wife Siobhan for her support, interest and encouragement and to my children (Greg, Kim, Devon, Maryn and Dylan) to whom this book is dedicated. May they always enjoy the "voices" of our writers.

Grant Holcomb
Rochester, New York
January 2001

Contents

Contents (continued)

Artwork

Introduction

During my fifteen-year tenure as Director of the Memorial Art Gallery, I have developed a profound respect for the cultural heritage of western New York. The region has been the home of Elbert Hubbard and The Roycrofters, as well as the brothers Stickley. The New York State College of Ceramics at Alfred University and the School for American Crafts at the Rochester Institute of Technology remain preeminent in their respective fields. Rochester itself has a rich diversity of cultural institutions. As a "music city" it has, among others, the Hochstein School of Music, the Rochester Philharmonic Orchestra and the inimitable Eastman School of Music of the University of Rochester. It is the home of such singular museums as the George Eastman House (International Museum of Photography and Film), the Strong Museum and the nearby Genesee Country Museum and Village. The internationally acclaimed Garth Fagan Dance is yet another jewel in the cultural crown of the city.

Of course the region also has a vibrant literary tradition. Shortly upon my arrival in Rochester, I learned not only that the noted poet John Ashbery was born in the city but that he even took art classes in the Gallery's Creative Workshop. Later, as a board member of BOA Editions, the award-winning poetry publishing house, I became increasingly familiar with the literary richness of this area.

Grant Holcomb

(2001)

I then came across Edward Hirsch's book *Transforming Vision: Writers on Art*, a compilation of writings on the collection at The Art Institute of Chicago. That book, along with the good counsel and sustained support of Rochester poets William Heyen and Jarold Ramsey, encouraged me to put together a similar volume of writings on art by poets and novelists who have had connections to western New York State. The forty writers in this book were each asked to select a work of art from the permanent collection of the Memorial Art Gallery and respond with a poem, short story or essay. The responses were immediate and most gratifying, as the writers who appear in this book include Poet Laureates, Pulitzer Prize and National Book Award winners, New York State Poets and MacArthur Fellows.

Other museums have found that poems provide an opportunity to linger a bit longer in front of a work of art. The Art Institute of Chicago, The University of Michigan Museum of Art, The Tate Gallery and the Elvehjem Museum of Art at the University of Wisconsin, for example, have organized and published collaborations between "the sister arts." Ed Hirsch clearly stated the importance of these projects: the poet and novelist, he writes, "teach us to look and look again more closely. They dramatize with great intensity the actual experience of encounter." Those last five words underscore the challenge and the vision of all museum educators, curators and directors.

"Each work of art demands its response"

Valery

The encounter between poetry and painting has ancient roots, from the theories of Aristotle and Horace's famous phrase (*ut pictora poesis* or "as in painting, so in poetry") to Leonardo's concise statement that "Painting is poetry which is seen and not heard, and poetry is a painting which is heard but not seen." The intimate relationship among painting, poetry and calligraphy is found throughout Chinese culture. And was there ever a poet more obsessed with art than John Keats in nineteenth-century England? As one critic claimed, "We often feel, in Keats, that we are wandering through a museum, following…an eloquent and subtle guide." In nineteenth-century America, Emily Dickinson often connected poetry with painting in both her poems and letters, while Asher B. Durand paid homage to the kinship between painter (Thomas Cole) and poet (William Cullen Bryant) is his 1849 painting *Kindred Spirits*.

The visual image was a central component of much twentieth-century poetry. And, today, it is rare to pick up a volume of poetry and not find the poet responding to a work of art. Poet J. D. McClatchy notes that the twentieth century "is especially rich not only in poems that seek to 'resemble' imaginary pictures but also in poems that seek to interpret existing ones." Edward Hopper, for example, has long attracted the attention of contemporary poets. "Poets and storytellers/move into the vacancies/Edward Hopper left them," Lisel Mueller writes in her poem "American Literature," and Mark Strand insists that Hopper's work invites the poet "to construct a narrative for each painting…as part of the experience of looking."

At times, the poet becomes a docent, our guide through special exhibitions. Eamon Grennan's poems "Statue" and "Women Going," for example, respond to the 1993 exhibition *The Greek Miracle* at the National Gallery of Art. At other times, our poets have written insightful books on major American artists: Joyce Carol Oates on George Bellows; Mark Strand on Edward Hopper and William Bailey; Charles Simic on Joseph Cornell; and John Ashbery on Cornell, Jane Freilicher, Louisa Matthiasdottir and Henry Darger, to name but a few important contributions. We can even study painters who have written poetry (from Bronzino and Michelangelo to Fairfield Porter) and poets who have painted (from William Blake to e.e. cummings and Elizabeth Bishop).

McClatchy establishes that paintings, for most poets, "are primal, as 'real' as the bread and wine on the table, as urgent as a dying parent or concealed lover in the next room." The writer's response to art is equally urgent and significant for, as Seamus Heaney declared in his 1995 Noble Lecture, "images and stories…do function as bearers of value" in all societies.

Our forty writers, all with connections (past or present) to western New York, continue this long and complex relationship between the verbal and the visual. Their lucent and knowing responses range from the wild, humorous inventiveness of Charles Bernstein's poem "Slap Me Five, Cleo, Mark's History" to the gritty "hour of charcoal and amber" in Kate Braverman's response to Douglas Gorsline's 1942 painting *Bar Scene*. Cornelius Eady revels in the "July jazz, August's hot bop" of Jacob Lawrence's torrid *Summer Street Scene in Harlem*, while a nineteenth-century still life by Richard LaBarre Goodwin triggers a haunting childhood memory for Steve Huff. With Anthony Hecht, we travel with St. Paul on "The Road to Damascus" and learn of the "strange, confused accounts," while, with Ben Howard, we contemplate the "delicate but…decisive" hands of Abraham Lincoln that "keep their place amidst/the landscapes, the chat of passers-by." Winslow Homer's magnificent painting *The Artist's Studio in an Afternoon Fog* was singled out by three writers (distinctive poems by Susan Howe and Deborah Tall and a delightful short story by Tom Gavin). Several others were drawn to a notable group of nineteenth-century American landscape paintings that, as Jarold Ramsey writes, "began/to register the beauty and the virtue of this land." John Ashbery found the contemporary landscape painting by Jane Freilicher "a continual *joie de vivre.*" With imagination and originality, these writers have recreated the works of art and have enabled us to see anew many of the treasures in the collections of the Memorial Art Gallery.

Milton Avery

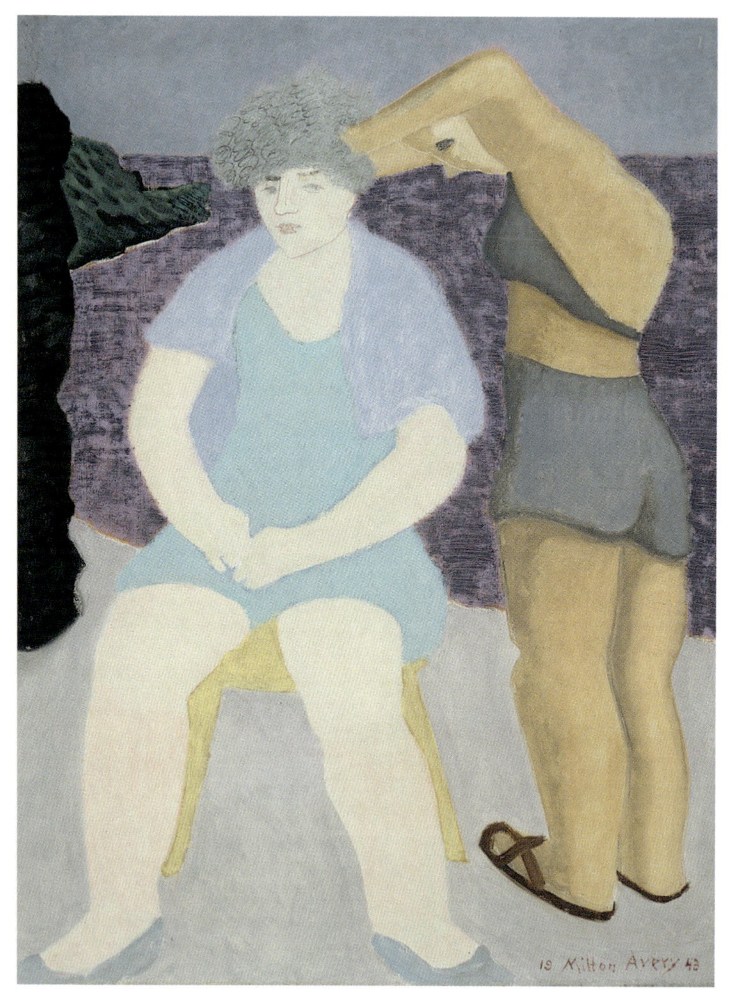

Haircut by the Sea

(1943)

Kath M. Anderson

She's in the sea of someone touching her

head, the light near-sleep of intentional

caress, past the scent of asphalt, lapis

petunias and bedsheets long overdue

for the wash. The sea behind her allows

for miles of generous prose without a

single story, giraffes swimming the sands,

long necks swaying in unison above

As Could the Sea

(2000)

Kath

M. Anderson

mists made purely of dust. Under the

purple wall of ocean, cobalt sea robins

swarm, and indigo octopus made of

jackballs and pipe cleaners. Beyond

the blue cave of her armpit, men are at

war. Her face is the porcelain limit

of conversation they do not cross—

her mother's lethally level-headed

compliments, some blues in the soothing

tempo of revision and tangent. She

leaves them all on the flat raft of the sea.

She could hear, if she chose, the hearts

of blue whales beating three miles out.

The frizzy cloud of her hair begins to

let go, as if evaporation were

one of her talents, an unrepentant

exclamation of weather. Soon the other

will dive into that seahair where thoughts stick

like chicory in the current of an

August haze, or unfold in the portion

of her mind she thought she'd given away

to a man. At any moment, either

woman could go wherever she wants.

As could the sea. As could the navy sky.

Jane Freilicher

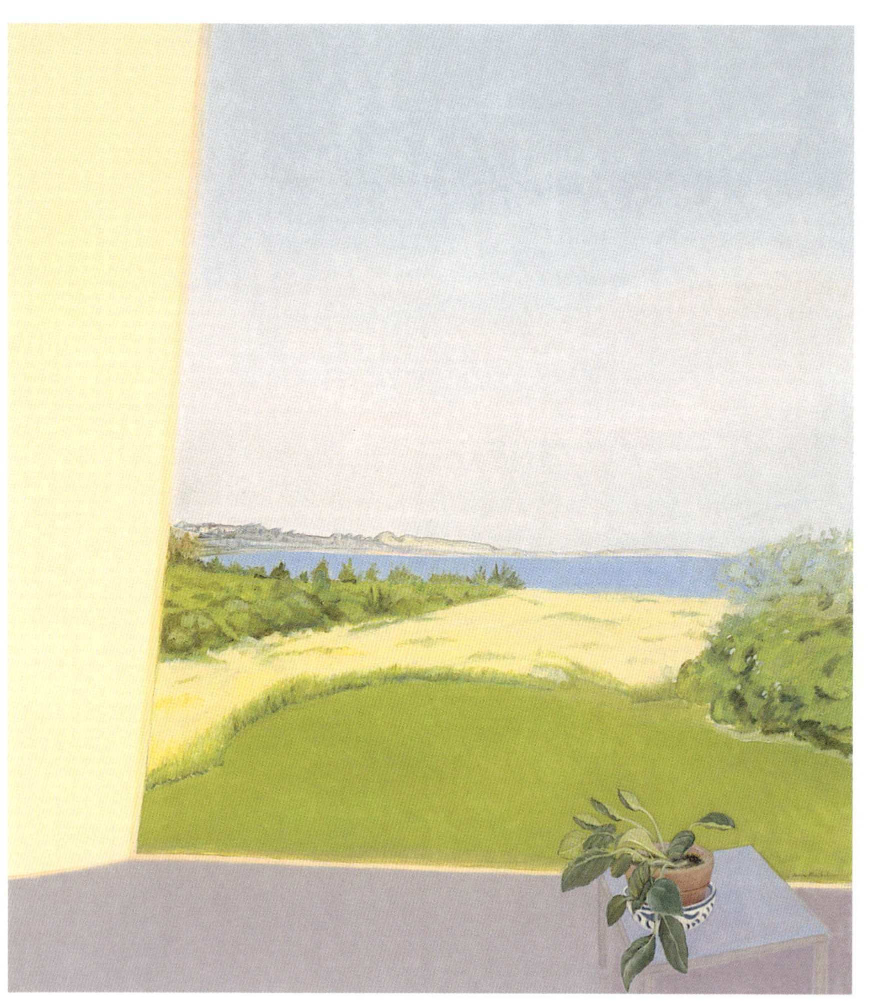

View Over Mecox (Yellow Wall)

(1991-1993)

John Ashbery

Throughout her long career, Jane Freilicher has always seemed equally fascinated by the medium she happens to be using and the prospect before her, which is frequently the same one: an interior or exterior view in her studios in New York and Water Mill, Long Island. (Not such a limited one in fact, since it can include the Atlantic Ocean and adjacent Mecox Bay, and the landscape of lower Manhattan, including glimpses of the Hudson River and the New Jersey heights beyond it, as well as the mysteriously luminous night sky over the city.) Still, her landscapes, like Courbet's forest scenes, seem less

Jane Freilicher: *View Over Mecox*

(2000)

John

Ashbery

interested in conveying a strong sense of genius loci than a

general sense of the components of landscape: grass in all its

grassiness, trees without the poetry of "Trees" but as objects in

the prospect, water that suggests the sweep but not necessarily

the skittering surface of, say, Mecox Bay. We have seen such

things countless times and don't need to be reminded of

how they looked at a specific moment. They are apprehended by

Freilicher somewhere between that moment and the

generalizations of eternity. Mecox Bay in her painting of it

bears a family resemblance to Mecox Bay the place, but the

family relationship isn't a very close one—more like that of

a first cousin once removed.

This may be due to a democratic urge to avoid the solemnity

of "privileged moments" in favor of a feeling for how nature and

objects just keep plugging along—it's that, perhaps, that

makes them ultimately important to us. And there is as well her

constant awareness of the materials she is using—oil (as here),

pastel, charcoal, whatever. The pigment that stands in for water

is as much an object of delectation as the water itself. It has to

be humored, nudged, helped along to awareness of its

materiality even if that means forgetting subject matter for a

moment. Of course she always returns to the subject—one can

even sense her taking a few steps backward toward the end of the

painting session, squinting to make sure it all checks out and

holding the brush horizontally to see how it compares to the

horizontality of the horizon. (If they don't quite match, that's

OK too.) The end result, for me, is a continual joie de vivre

whose source is light breaking out of the canvas, as though it had

filled every crevice to overflowing. The painting sings a song of

thingness, whether that of the swatch of nature sitting for its

portrait or the paint that's helping it to become itself even as it

casually poses for its own portrait.

Albert Bierstadt

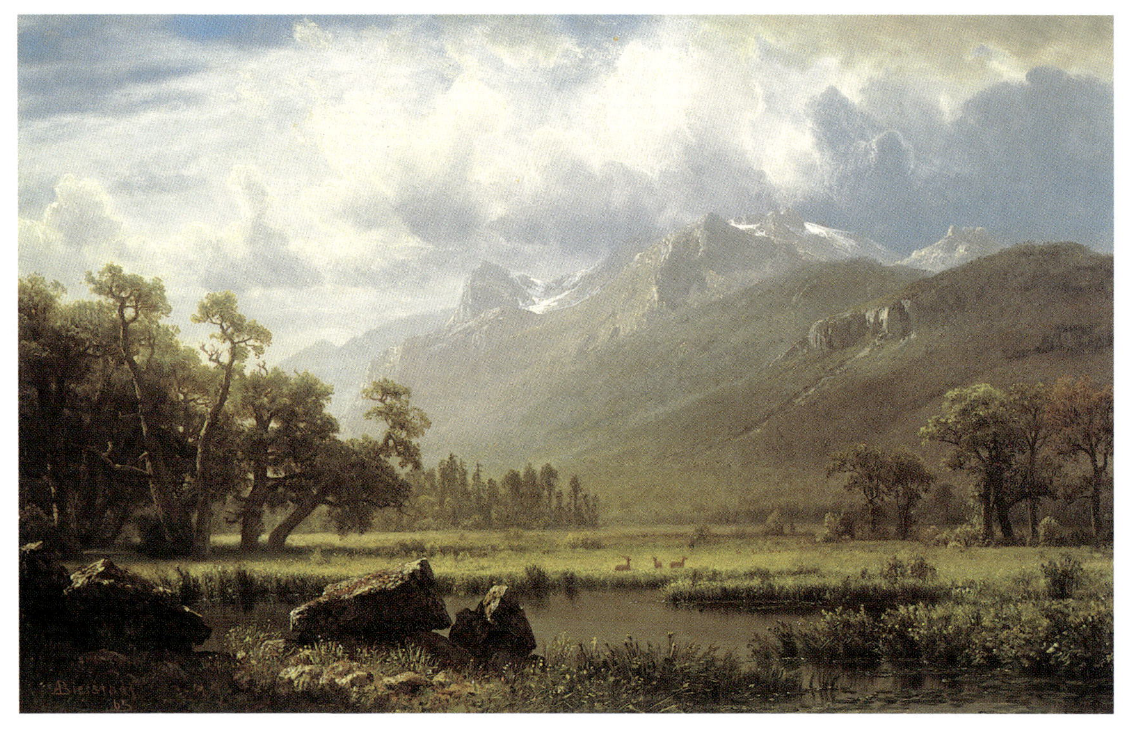

The Sierras Near Lake Tahoe, California

(1865)

John Frederick Kensett

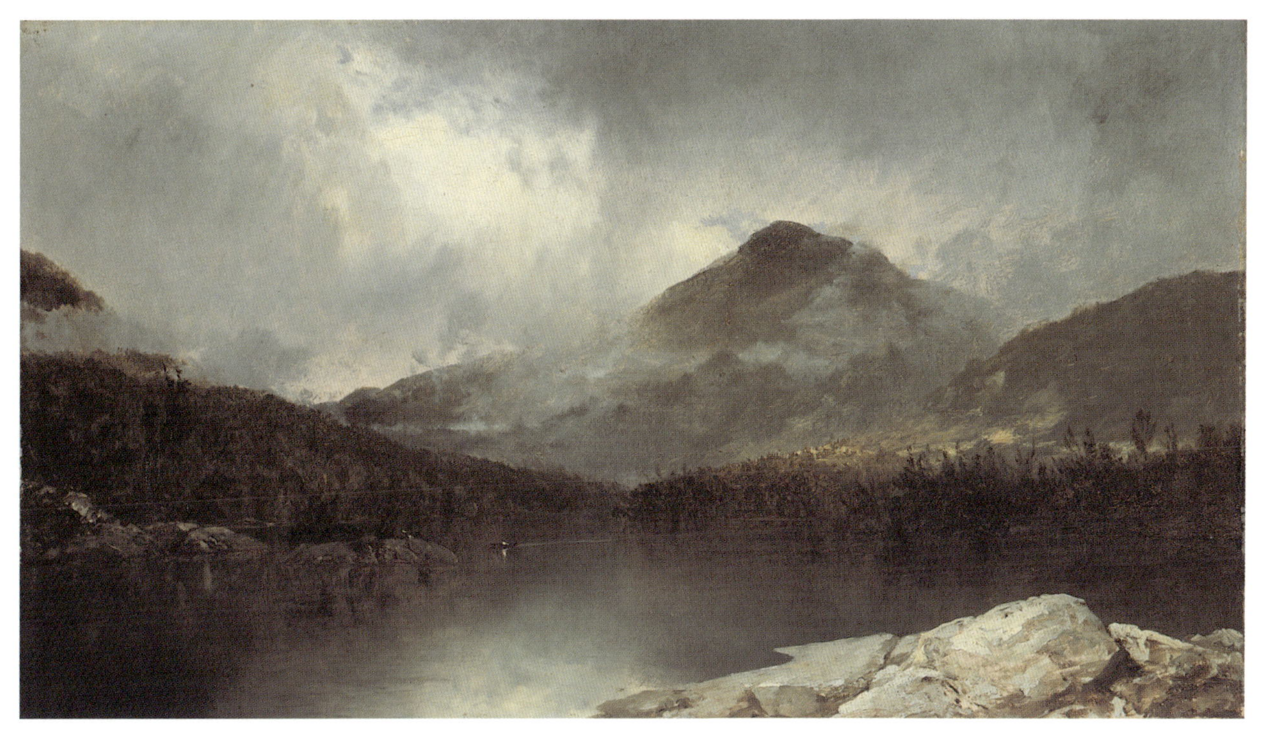

A Showery Day, Lake George

(ca. 1860)

Andrea Barrett

Why do these paintings look so much alike? Bierstadt's depicts a majestic mountain rising, just right of center, above a watery landscape rendered in misty olives and black and rust and brown. In the middle distance three tiny deer are barely visible; creamy clouds roll through a sky more gray than blue. Specks of brilliant white—flowers, foam?—dot the shallow foreground. Kensett's depicts a majestic mountain rising, just right of center, above the olive and black and rust and brown shores of a gleaming dark lake. In the middle distance a tiny boat drifts, barely visible; misty gray clouds hang in a gray sky. White specks—in the boat, on an island—might be human beings. In both paintings the mountains seem unimaginably far away: to be longed for, but perhaps never reached.

The Middle Distance

(2000)

The exaggerated scale and depth of field suit Bierstadt's vast Sierras—but I once spent a summer at Lake George, netting and dissecting fish, and I remember no place like Kensett's vision. I saw low clouds, long rains, dark hills looming over the water, which was rimmed by summer cabins. Hunched over heaps of yellow perch, trying to understand one component of that late twentieth-century concept called an ecosystem, I felt enclosed by the mountains, almost stifled. I had none of the nineteenth-century sense of that landscape as spiritual event, and would never have seen it as equivalent to an enormous range on the other side of the country.

The exaggerated scale and depth of field suit Bierstadt's vast Sierras—but I once spent a summer at Lake George, netting and dissecting fish, and I remember no place like Kensett's vision. I saw low clouds, long rains, dark hills looming over the water, which was rimmed by summer cabins. Hunched over heaps of yellow perch, trying to understand one component of that late twentieth-century concept called an ecosystem, I felt enclosed by the mountains, almost stifled. I had none of the ninteenth-century sense of that landscape as spiritual event, and would never have seen it as equivalent to an enormous range on the other side of the country.

But in the conjunction of these views—they hang just a few feet apart now, and were painted at almost the same time—is a particularly sharp example of the way paintings can illuminate the past. When I'm writing fiction set in other times, I like to look at paintings like these. Although they aren't necessarily accurate transcriptions of particular sites they are, perhaps more usefully and importantly, representations of how people *thought*. This pair's kinship of composition and palette and tone reflects a kinship of vision and feeling.

What they say to me is not, Lake George looked like this in the 1860s, and the Sierras looked like that. They say, together, that to those two painters in that time, mountains are majestic, the sky leads to heaven, the water is dark and secret and deep and conceals great mysteries. They say that, amid such grandeur, painter and viewer alike are infinitely tiny; even the deer are almost lost. They say that to those men, in that time of Civil War, the wilderness appeared dense and shadowed, occluded in part, yet also capable of being opened by heaven's light. Perhaps they say that nature is beautiful, if the human beings are removed.

What Kensett's painting, in particular, says to me is that his view of Lake George was influenced by the same assumptions about the relative power of wilderness and civilization that are apparent in the colossal scale of Bierstadt's western landscapes. To me, now, Lake George seems tame, completely surrounded; the mountains look like hills and civilization appears to have conquered. But my own assumptions are no more transparent than Kensett's, and have colored the way I see the place. In Kensett's painting I can see the way it looked to him, then: a window into his mind, into his time.

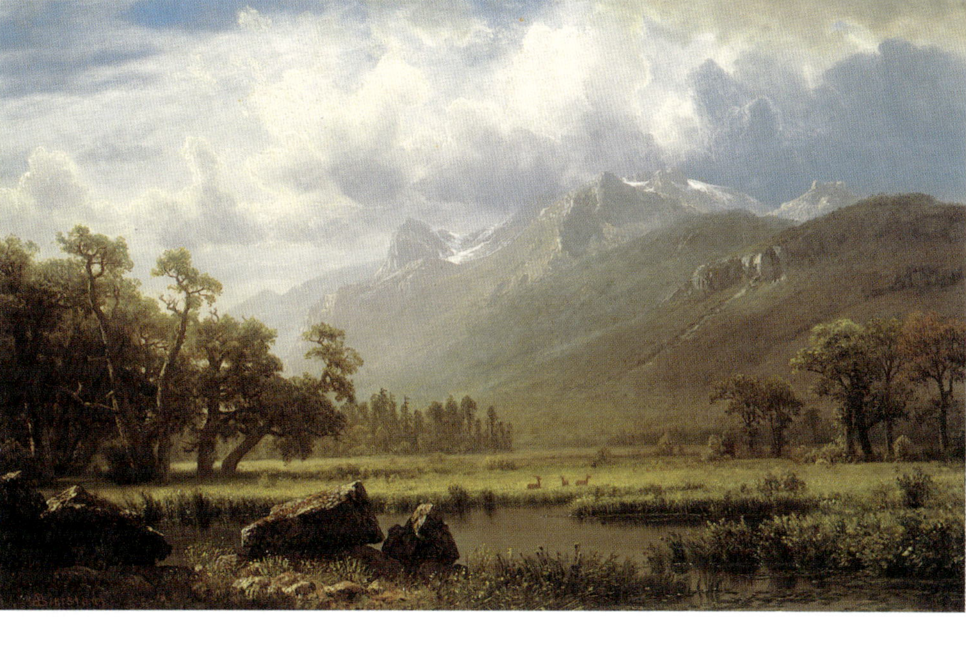

31

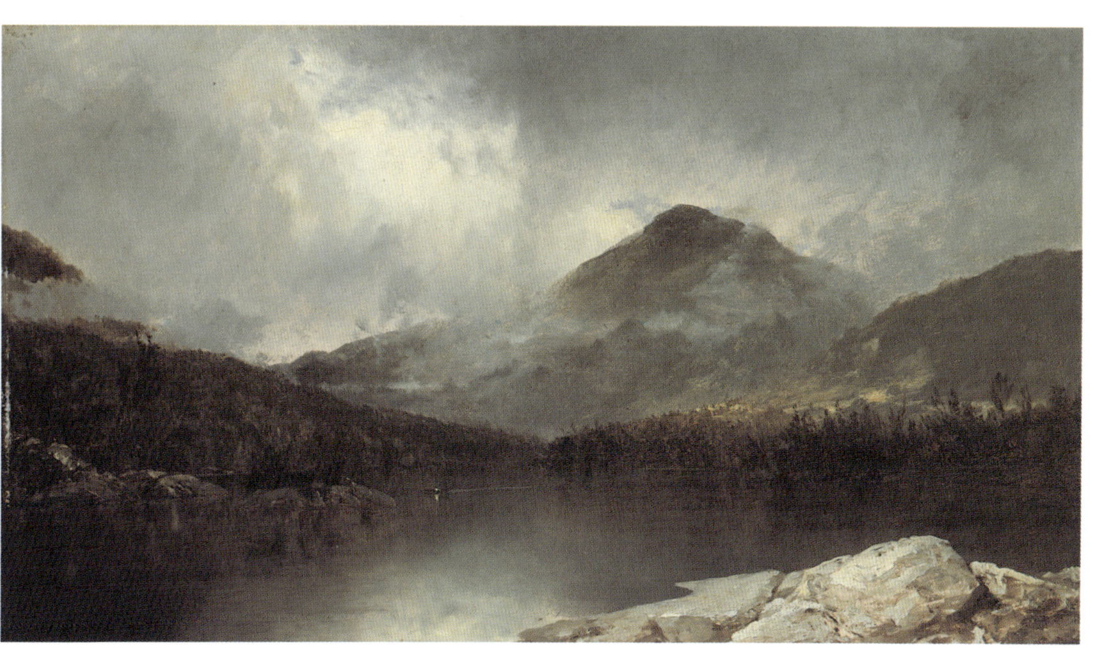

Ralph Albert Blakelock

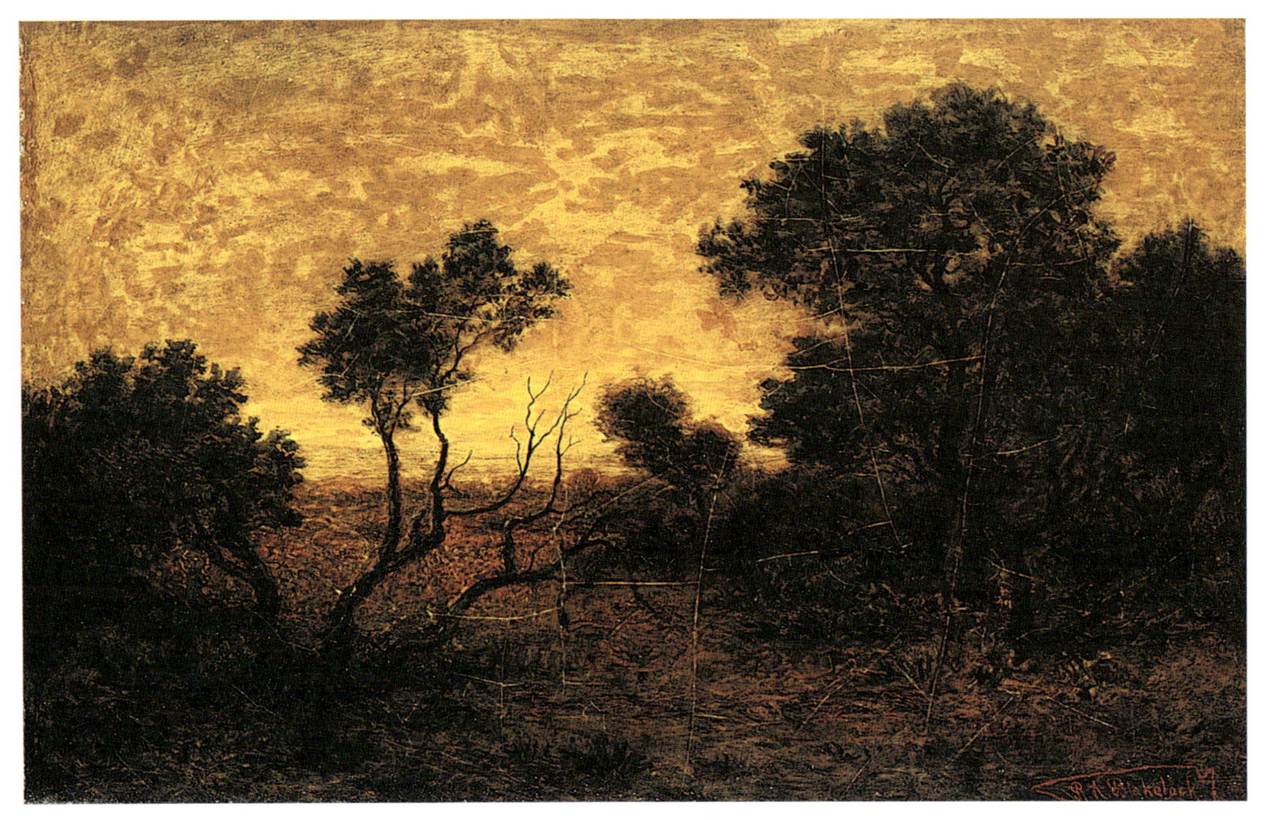

Landscape with Trees

(ca. 1880)

Todd Beers

Two days
later
the tree
still bows
in the
brown sky
before
pheasants
wake a
brief clear-
ing in
the ab-
sence of
human
voices.

Ralph Blakelock's *Landscape with Trees*

(2000)

Paul Klee

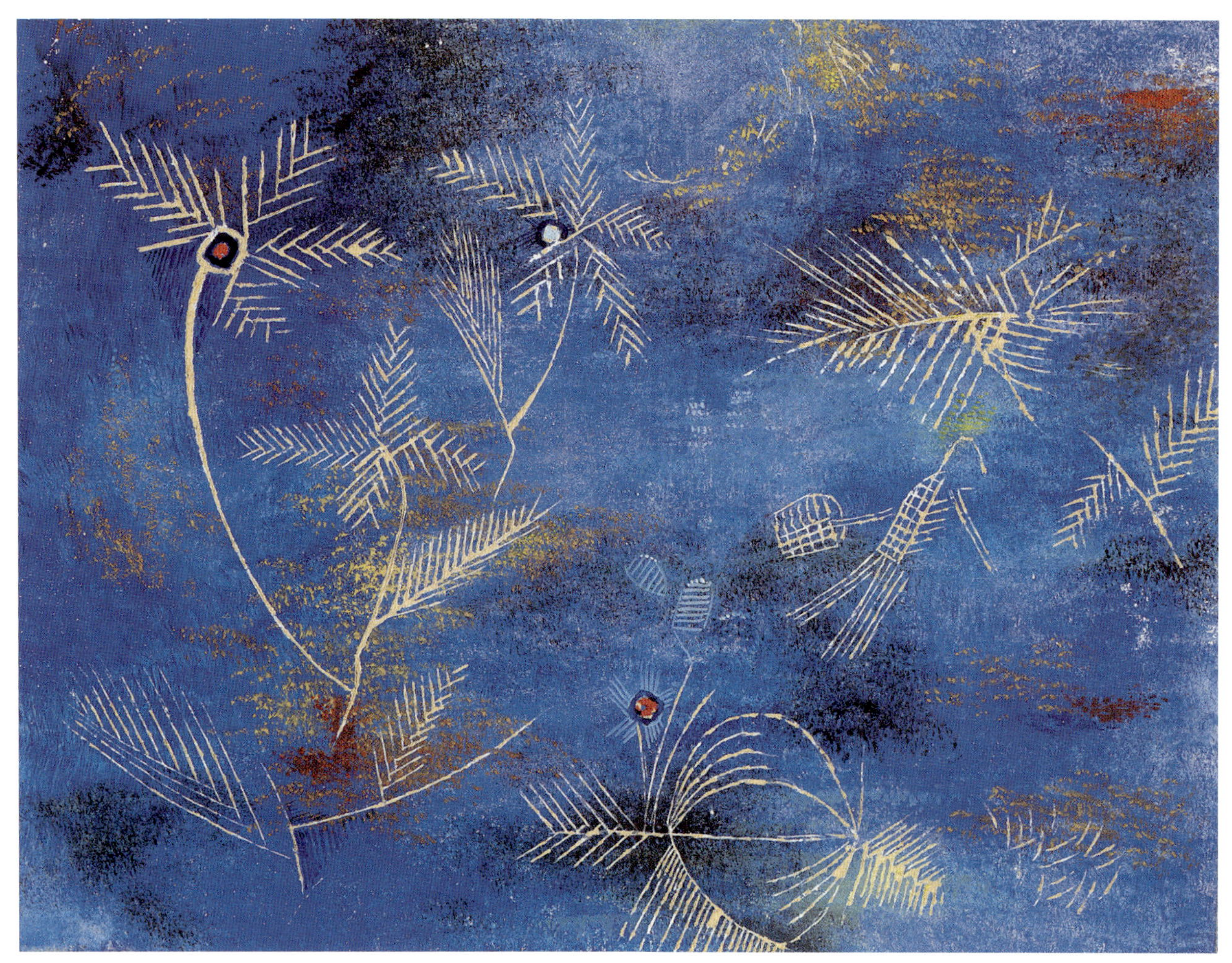

Fairy Tales

(ca. 1920)

Marvin Bell

There was a boy who took a poke at Heaven.

Then the sky filled up with flowers, pinwheels!

To reach them, all he had to do was climb

Upward in his head while he was sleeping.

The leaves fell upward, too, and there they stuck.

There, it was blue, with a touch of ruby sunset.

The blue the robin shatters, being born.

The blue that calms a child swept from its bed.

Paul Klee Tells His Story to the Children

(2000)

He thought: "Someday when I am taller, older,

I will teach my hands to feel upward, like a tree.

I will find the red thread that leads to Heaven,

And keep all the string I used afloat about me."

From a blue boyhood, he rose as a leaf falls.

With airy fins and feathers, with sticks and stones.

And he brought trees that live on air to leave.

He spoke with agile hands, with wingèd fingers.

In the cloud-splashed sky, he sketched a story.

He painted fish and flowers, and always himself.

He painted quickly, knowing the stain of sunset.

His paintings have the feeling of dreams come true.

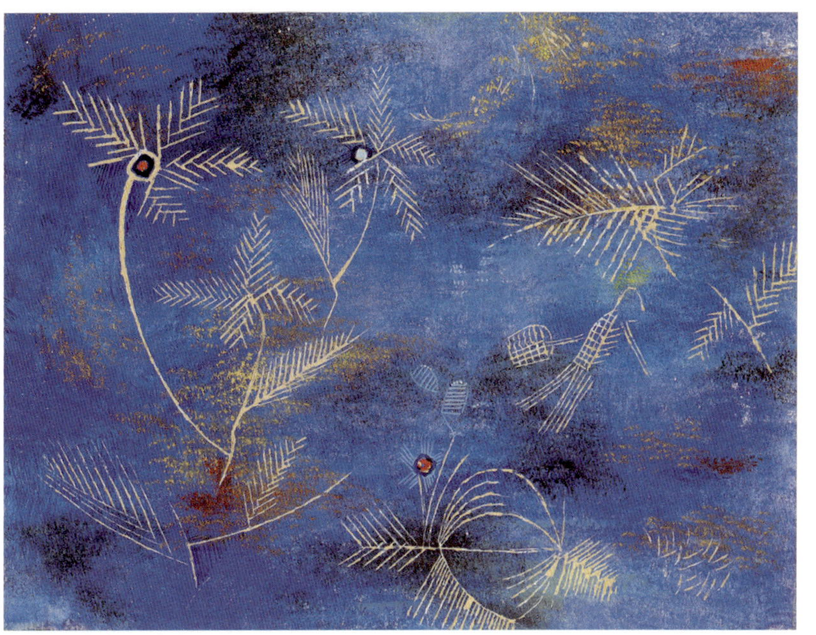

Ralston Crawford

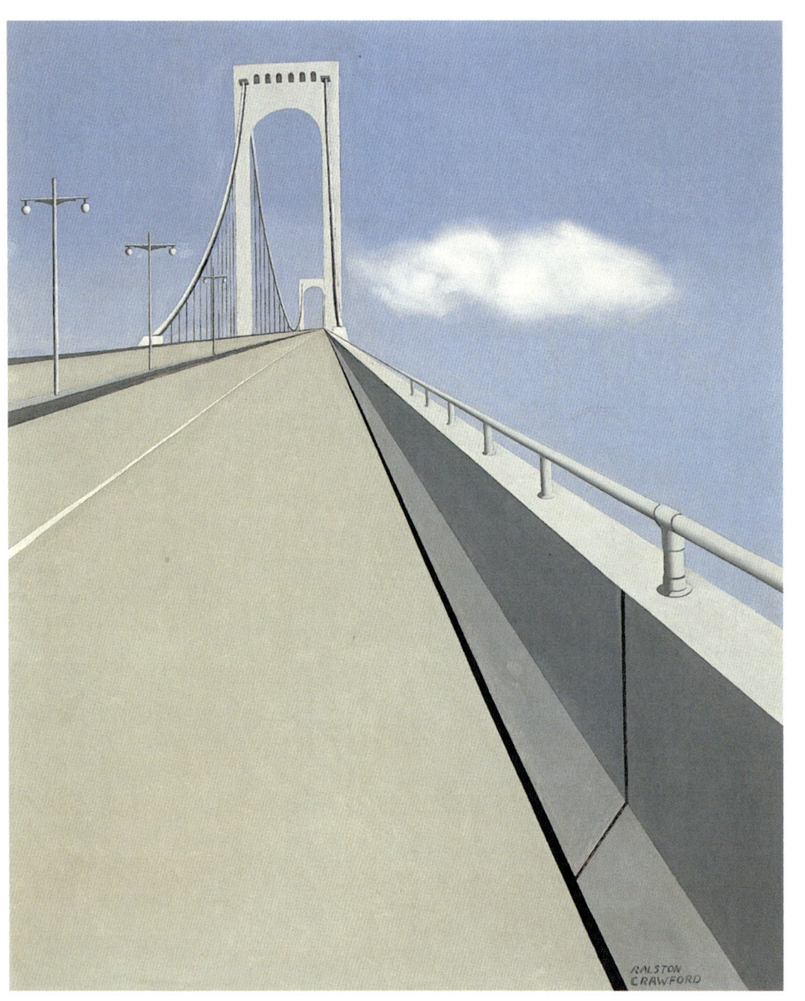

Whitestone Bridge

(1939)

Edwin Dickinson

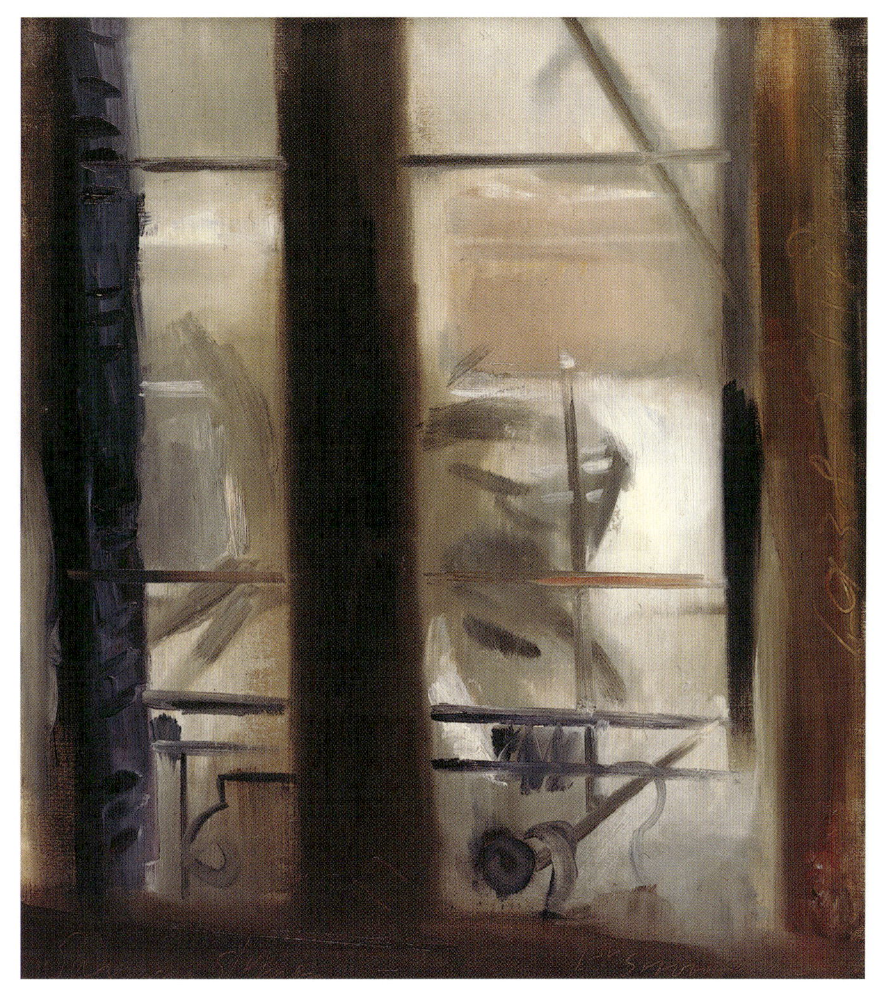

Snow on Quai, Sanary

(1938)

Wayne Thiebaud

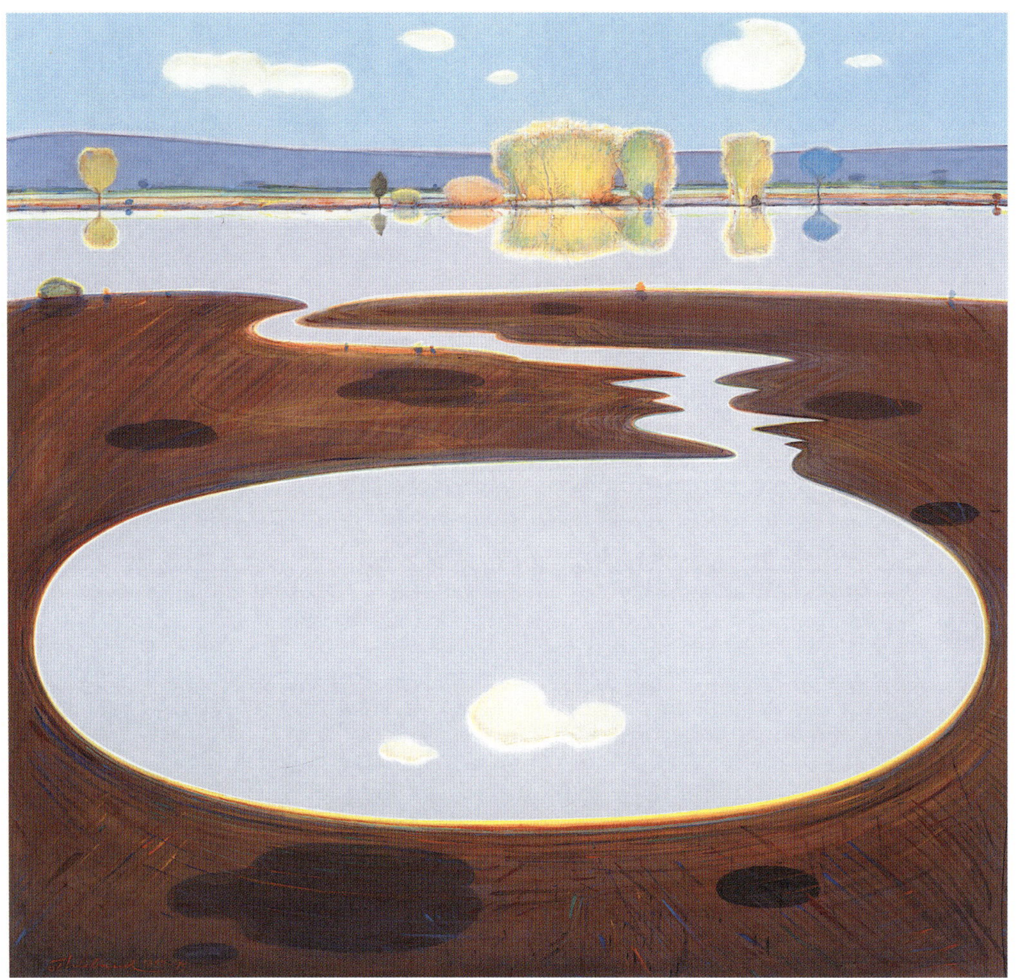

Wayne Thiebaud, *River Pond*, 1967-1975. © Wayne Thiebaud/Licensed by VAGA, New York, NY.

River Pond

(1967-1975)

Bruce Bennett

I. *Whitestone Bridge*

Ralston Crawford

II. *Snow on Quai, Sanary*

Edwin Dickinson

III. *River Pond*

Wayne Thiebaud

As in a dream, the empty span

climbs skyward, ending in the blue;

a trailing cloud, off to the right,

the only other thing in view,

adds to the giddy sense of height

and nothingness, as if one can,

by letting go, float out of sight.

But here one's caught. The frame is set:

a solid scene beyond the pane,

a cityscape of sorts – and yet,

it's all ablur; is that a train

or building in the background? Snow

has fallen and is falling. Whoa!

Is that a horse? (Or, if not, what?)

We're somewhere we have never been;

the colors are too clean, too bright,

the sky and water too pristine.

One tree's an eerie blue. The light

shimmers, and on the water's sheen,

recumbent, floating at our feet,

drift high clouds that cannot be seen.

Perspectives: A Triptych

(2000)

Bernard Duvivier

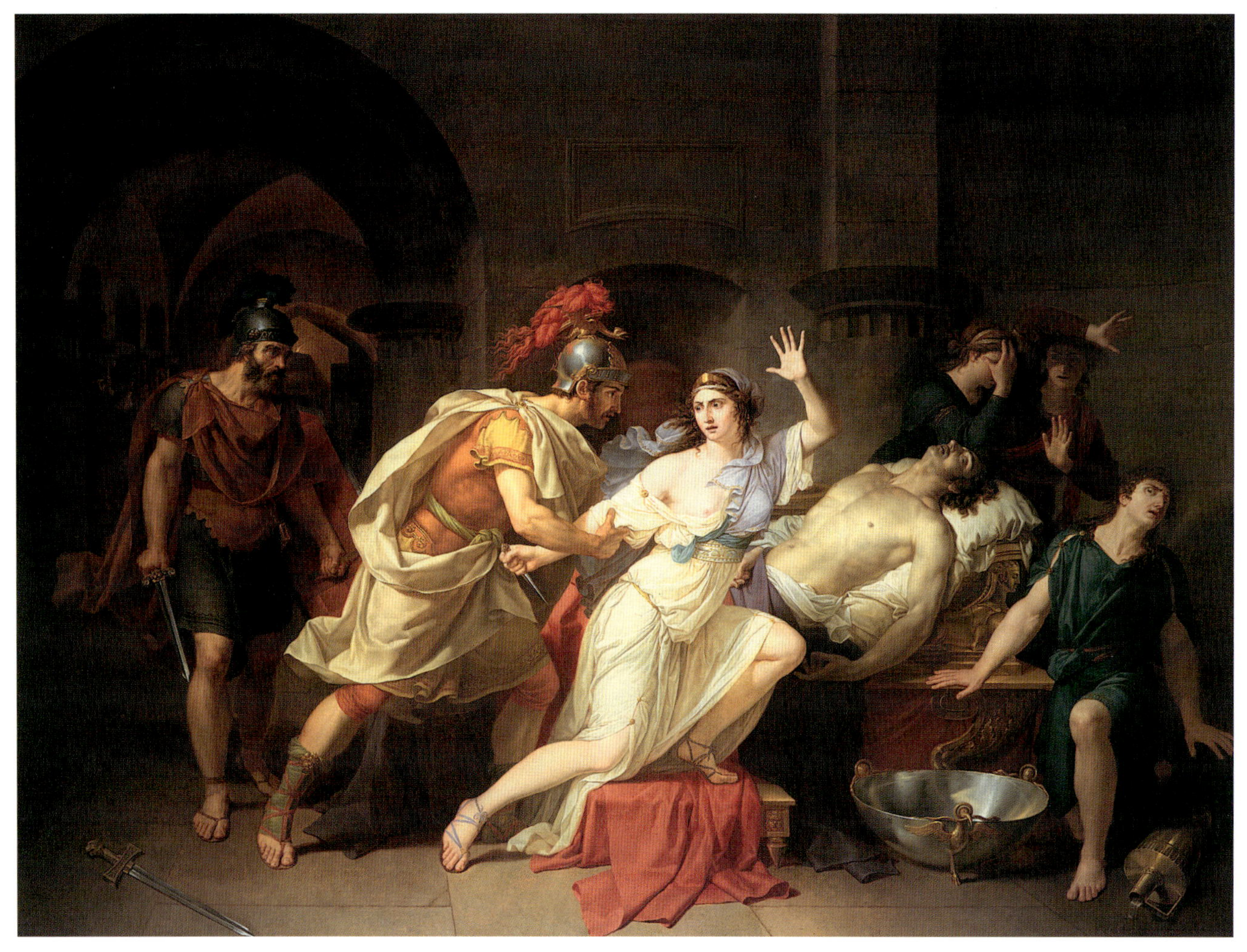

Cleopatra Captured by Roman Soldiers

(1789)

Charles Bernstein

Hello, my name is Michael Anthony

and I have in my hand a cashier's check

for one million dollars made out

in your name. There are no conditions

on the use of this money. You can spend it

any way you want, even give some to

the Memorial Art Gallery, which needs

your support, but you know that. Donations

to the Poetics Program at the University

at Buffalo are also welcome, and for

donations of $500 or more we will include

you or your loved ones in our poems, or,

if you prefer, we can compose more poems

relating to this painting or other paintings

in the collection. – But hold on a minute,

I'm getting ahead of myself. Let me

back up. There is one condition on the million:

you are not allowed to reveal the name

of the benefactor. If I tell you his name,

I'm counting on you to keep it to yourself.

Anyway, maybe you've already guessed

that it's John Beresford Tipton. You'd

Slap Me Five, Cleo, Mark's History

(2000)

know the name if you watched *The Millionaire*
on TV in the 1950s. (I don't think the show's
made it yet to "Nick at Night" or "TV Land,"
but then I don't follow their programming
that closely. But I'm sure not getting
residuals, that money dried up a long time
ago.) Of course a million isn't what it used
to be, but what is? Anyway, you know, enough
about me. You didn't invite me here to talk
about myself, well *you* didn't invite me here
at all. So let's get on to the subject at hand,
because we haven't got all day. We see before
us Bernard Duvivier's *Cleopatra. – Hey,*
Jimmy! Get up from the bench, take the
headphones off, and come over here
or you won't be going to the roller rink later!
(Excuse me, I hope it won't be necessary
to interrupt this poem again, so everybody
pay attention.) *Cleopatra* is dated 1789,
the year of the French Revolution, so we
must first consider how this painting relates
to the momentous events of that fateful year,
for a painting is never just about its ostensive
subject but always contains within it another,
often unseen, often contradictory, subject,
played out in its form or figured in its
imagery. In this case, we must assume

some historically specific reference, some
sign of the revolution taking place
outside the artist's studio. And yet, it's
hard to see what that would be. Could it be
that Antony and Cleopatra in some way
stand for characters from the contemporary
historical drama of 1789? Cleopatra is no
Marie Antoinette, I can tell you that,
and Antony, well he's no Louis XVI,
as I am sure you would agree
if you knew Louis like I know Louis –
O! What a guy! I mean human character
is something I specialize in. And I know
Louis and Marie, not just the cardboard
images out of books but the real flesh
and blood people. Just last week, Louis,
Marie, and I had a knockout lunch with
Jack Tipton at Montrachet – the frogs legs
were delicious, crisp as a Lay's potato
chip and coated with a dazzling avocado
meringue sauce. And the patisserie
was out-of-this-world. "Let us eat ze cake,"
Louis joked, always the wise guy, but
you should have seen the look on Marie's
face: she was not amused. It was nice of
Tippy to pick up the check as the French
royals have been having a hard time

the past couple of hundred years. I mean
whether you agree with them or not, you've
got to respect the tradition they represent.
No, if we are to look for allegory in this
painting, we have to think of something
different, something more off the mark.
Perhaps the symbolic potential of middle-aged
lovers defying society? Cleopatra and Antony
look very youthful for 39 and 53 – and this
is way before vitamin supplements, too.
But, let's face it, this is no Citizen Cleo
taking up arms against the old order
in the name of liberty, equality, and
fraternity. Whatever virtues the pair
may have, democracy is no part of them.
Fraternization maybe, but that's it. Duvivier
shows Cleopatra with a knife, ready to end
this mortal coil and join her beloved in that
better place just outside the frame. This is not
a revolutionary gesture but rather an
inwardly directed act of violence, suggesting
severe depression at the acute loss of a loved
one in a person without the emotional resources
to go through the grieving process and end up
a stronger, healthier, more self-empowered
individual. Such images of self-directed violence
have been shown, time and again, to have

a harmful effect on viewers, especially
a painting like this, which romanticizes suicide.
Paintings with this type of subject matter
should be restricted to patrons over 30
who can demonstrate their emotional maturity;
my only reservation about this course
of action is that it would only draw more
attention to this reprehensible glorification
of self-slaughter. – I hope you will allow
me to indulge in a personal note here.
The shame of Mark's suicide has haunted
the Antony family for generations, so much so
that when emigrating from Italy in the 1880s,
my parents changed the spelling of our
name, adding an "h" for our missing honor.
And, speaking of families, what of Mark's first
family – Octavia and the children? Sure Queen
Cleopatra is sad, but what about them?
I wouldn't waste all your tears on Cleo.
Don't get me wrong, I understand what it's
like to be so low you think down is up. After
our show passed on – I mean was canceled, I
still have a hard time saying that word – I fell into
a downward spiral until I hit bottom at a dive
called At Our Place on the Bowery. That's
where I met Louis, who always wore a green
ribbon around his neck, although he would

Charles
Bernstein

never talk about it. Tippy tried to do what he could, offered to cover my stay at the Betty Ford clinic, but I had too much pride to accept his offer. Eventually I landed a job as research assistant to a young scholar associated with UB's Poetics Program, who specialized in poems about paintings and was at the time working on French neo-Classicism à la Jacques Louis David. Anyway, and correct me if I'm wrong, didn't Cleopatra do herself in with an asp shortly after the scene depicted in this painting? When she realized that the hundreds-year-old Ptolemaic dynasty would come to an end and Rome would rule Egypt? When push comes to shove, it wasn't romance that was on the Queen's mind, but the imminent political catastrophe for her country. Maybe that event was to be the subject of a sequel, ready to go into production if this painting hit big box office. Anyway, not to change the subject, but, and check this out – don't you think Antony looks more like he was caught in flagrante delicto than that he's dead? I guess that's poetic license (how do you apply for one of those?). Alas, none of us brings a blank slate, a tabula rasa, an unprejudiced gaze, to the reception of such an historically charged subject. For example, many contemporary viewers will have

foremost in their minds the comparison between the star-crossed lovers in this painting and their representation in Joseph L. Mankiewicz's 1963 film version of *Cleopatra*, starring Elizabeth Taylor and Richard Burton, with Rex ("Dr. Doolittle") Harrison as Julie Caesar. (Many people think of Julie only as a take-charge military commander and forget that he was the inspiration for that great vocal standard, "Roman Nights of an Egyptian Queen [Cleo's Song]" –"You came, you saw, you conquered me.") I cannot emphasize enough that in order to properly understand Duvivier's painting on its own terms, it is necessary to clear the mind of all such overlaid images. Try to put yourself in the position of the first viewers of this painting, who knew nothing of Liz and Dick's shenanigans in Rome, nor of the trials of Eddie Fisher. Such contemporary images put a cloud between us and this painting, a cloud that we can only hope to vaporize by rigorous analysis both of the painting itself and the historical reality of that August day, 30 years before the start of the first millennium, when people were just beginning to face the issues around Y-zero-K (ignition, lift-off). Let us then return to this painting, with a renewed

commitment to plumb its depth, scale its heights,
assay its thematics. No consideration of this work
would be anything but superficial if it considered
only the main actors in the unfolding drama
and overlooked the supporting cast. Let us then
turn our attention to Faith, Hope, and Larry –
the threesome just behind the stiff. Now Faith,
Faith looks like she's got Excedrin headache #49,
if not a migraine (but this was before product
placements and let me emphasize that there
are only minimal fees being paid for brand name
references in this poem). Hope seems to be
rehearsing for a Martha Graham revival. And
Larry – the guy in the lower right hand corner –
it looks like he's trying out an early version
of aerobics – "Get that knee up, all the way
up. Stretch those arms." But here's the weirdest
thing: Larry, let's call him Larry, bears an
uncanny resemblance to John Beresford Tipton.
I mean Jack Tipton always wore a suit, but
the guy in the picture has the same nose,
the same eyes, the same build. I mean explain
that. But I see I am letting the main emotional
action of the painting get away from me:
you know, the deep gaze being exchanged
by the Queen and the Roman guard Proculeius
(whose name we now associate primarily with

a common skin rash exacerbated by oil paint).
I mean, first Julius Caesar, then 'Tony, and
now … ? After all, who could resist a man
in a red dress wearing a helmet bedecked
with a long red feather? Or would you call
that a plume? I'd call it a feather but then
what do I know? I've never even been to
Egypt and I only took one summer of Latin
when I was in high school. "Julius Caesar
crossed the Rubicon." You can say that
double for Mark Antony. And while we are
on the subject, make mine a double, too,
with a twist. *That's right, double or nothing,
twist and shout, but be home by 11.* Now,
before we move on to the next painting,
I want you all to notice that Proculeius's
head accessories are so much more appealing
than the rubberbanded pony tail and baseball
cap now standard for balding men of my
generation – *no offense intended to you, sir,
yes you, looking away, with the bib overalls –*
but then perhaps Proculeius has one of those
pony tails tucked away under his helmet.
(Perhaps an x-ray of the painting is in order.)
And, hey, what's that? A miniature dragon
under the plumage? That's so cool. Anyway,
one thing's for sure, Cleopatra's sandals
are still very chic.

Douglas Warner Gorsline

48

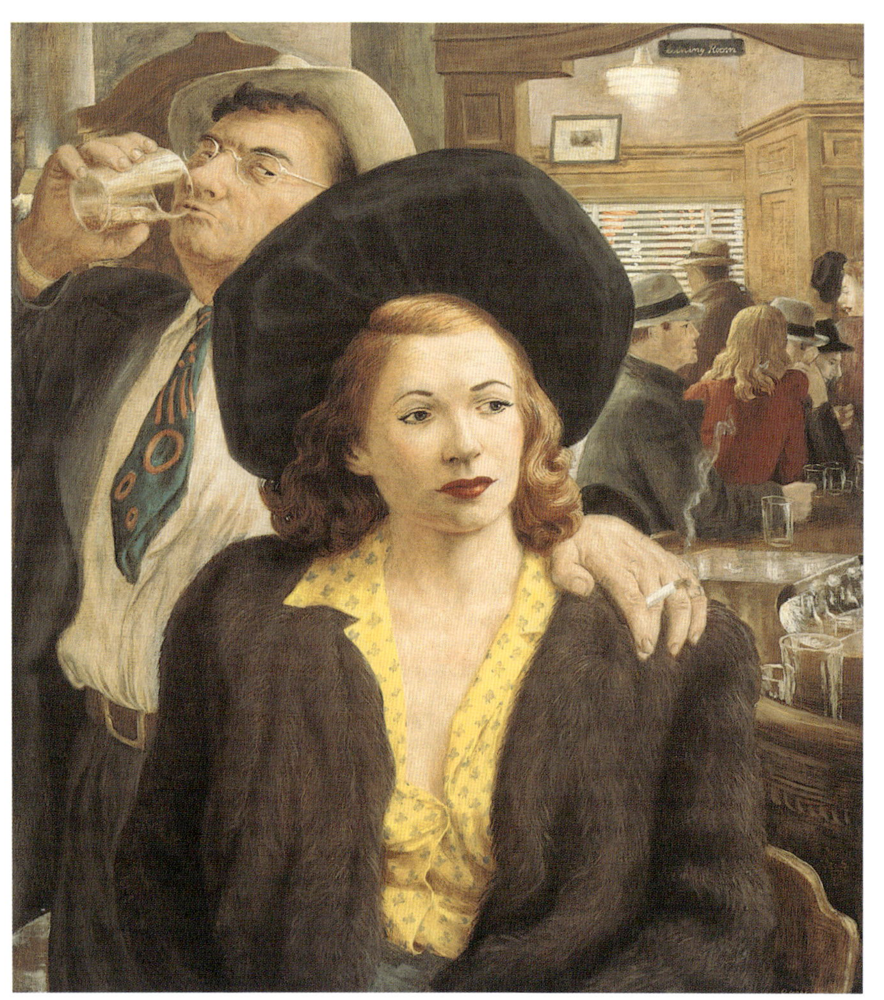

Bar Scene

(1942)

Kate Braverman

It is always the hour of charcoal and amber. There is a war
and it is fall. The leaves are like kissed mouths in the
gutter. The street is a shudder of October, skinned trees,
allies lit in reverse, illumination rising from concrete. Back
home, there would be swaying of half naked maples, bruised
martyrs smelling of pumpkin and tea rose. That has nothing
to do with you.

In this bar, the air is filtered and reduced. You wear a
blouse the color of crushed daffodils. He puts his hand on
your shoulder, the hand with the cigarette, and you are

Bar Scene

(2000)

erased. If you could speak, you would say you see a piece of boulevard through blinds. You sense limbs like lanterns at eye level, the wind is a sequence of flawed kimonos, autumn is shawled, but how can you know this? You haven't even been to Ohio.

The world is a terminal, a lottery and you paint your lips a magenta well between the tickets you buy. There is too much gray. Air is the texture of metal, bad food, child abuse and felonies. If you were to open your mouth, pewter would fall into your lungs. It's not the bullets, you think, but the caliber of the lie.

You have seen October thin like a woman with leukemia. There's a pause, a flinty antique ivory and then silence, the carcasses of sunflowers, the moon on another channel and no ropes. It would take a thousand years to explain this.

Yes, you want another drink. Yes, you always look sad, don't worry. You manage to say this to the man. A whistle outside, the end of the shift. A siren. You hear the church bells and they sound like a lash. You suspect you don't believe in god and that you don't trust anyone. Last night, wind was like a contained ocean eating at its borders. It felt like charged pewter or a sheet of aluminum. Your mouth tasted of tin.

He asks what you are thinking. You shrug your shoulder, under the old mink jacket borrowed from your roommate. You look out the place where a window should be. You think you could navigate by smell. Your head aches. It's another version of a dream your father once told you, tattooing your ears. It was like a slap on your face. It was a defining gesture. Now you wear your map on the outside. And sin is too small a concept. Night turns brutal, feral, with a hint of chipped enamel, birches fluttering like scorched gloves. Yes, you tell the man. You will go to his room, after another drink.

It is a stasis of stalled twilight. You remember mother. The hour when answers became red like the check for wrong spelling in third grade you never forgot. Mother is a confederation of wounds. She nourishes them, like kitchen philodendron. They are the secret silver service she polishes and shines. People have to die for you to get these objects. Cancer. Insanity. Radiation. Hitler. A bad divorce. Then we use the dish to be festive. It's a holiday tray to slice chocolate cake and pecan pie. No wonder so many old women eat alone, die alone, with their tarnished tea sets with tiny pink roses. They have a parrot in a cage. They tell it, you're a bad boy. Somebody should set you on fire.

It is time to drink and pretend you are happy. Lamplight settles on your skin like mustard gas. You consider the new poisons, more subtle than arsenic. Entire rows of men collapse. It is more efficient than hanging. And you can't remember this man's name or why such syllables should matter. You keep changing yours, giving yourself the name of flowers and movie stars and saints. You are Iris and Joan, Barbara Rose, Marlene. You change the spelling with a lilac pen when you should be typing. This age is about aliases and atoms, code names and elaborate subterfuge. You need a password for the bus. No one taught you this vocabulary. Now you have fallen behind.

His hand is like a bridge over your back, a metal claw, an artifact from the front. Everyone knows this is a moment of history. There are coffins in the boulevard the color of bleached cedar and bedside lamps burning out in back rooms. He asks what you are thinking. You are considering methods by which we learn blindness and how he could kiss you with his teeth, but that wouldn't be enough.

Now comes rain. You would like to talk about water. How you wish you could see the ocean, rivers beyond the Mohawk and Genesee. The rain is a form of terror. If it rained on your face, your skin would disintegrate, like the Jewish women in lime trenches someone on the radio talked about. You believe this can happen in Europe. Why not? After all, Rochester is a death camp, though they call it New York.

When he says it is time to leave, you will walk off the edge of the world. Everyone has tattoos, hieroglyphs on their flesh. You are thinking of anchors and water in wells and oceans. You are thinking of the drowned women from ferries and torpedoed boats that float at your feet, blue as monk's hood and larkspur. This is the residue, what fell from bridges, slid from riverbanks, the Ganges you have never seen, the Thames, the Mississippi.

He says, you're so quiet, you a war widow, maybe? Your boyfriend over there? Your lips are paralyzed. It's like a spelling bee or arithmetic with boxes and triangles and X's. Aren't we all like formulas for a vast unknown that burns? Aren't our faces war zones, with shrapnel inside like bird nests and blueberries? She is thinking, if you ask me to smile again, I will show you lips pure as acid.

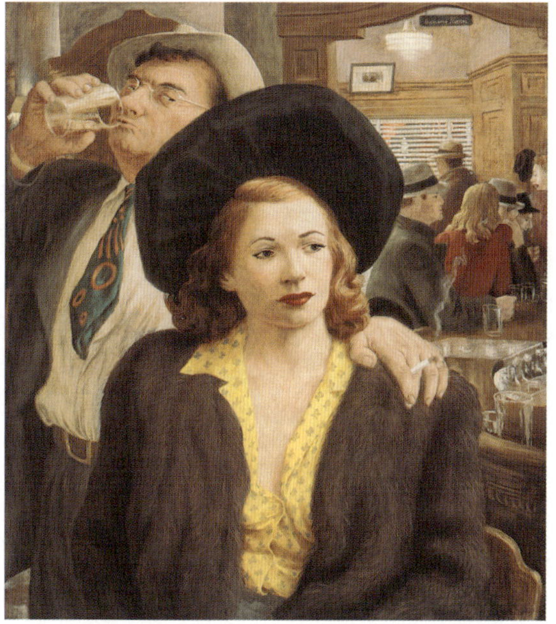

Winslow Homer

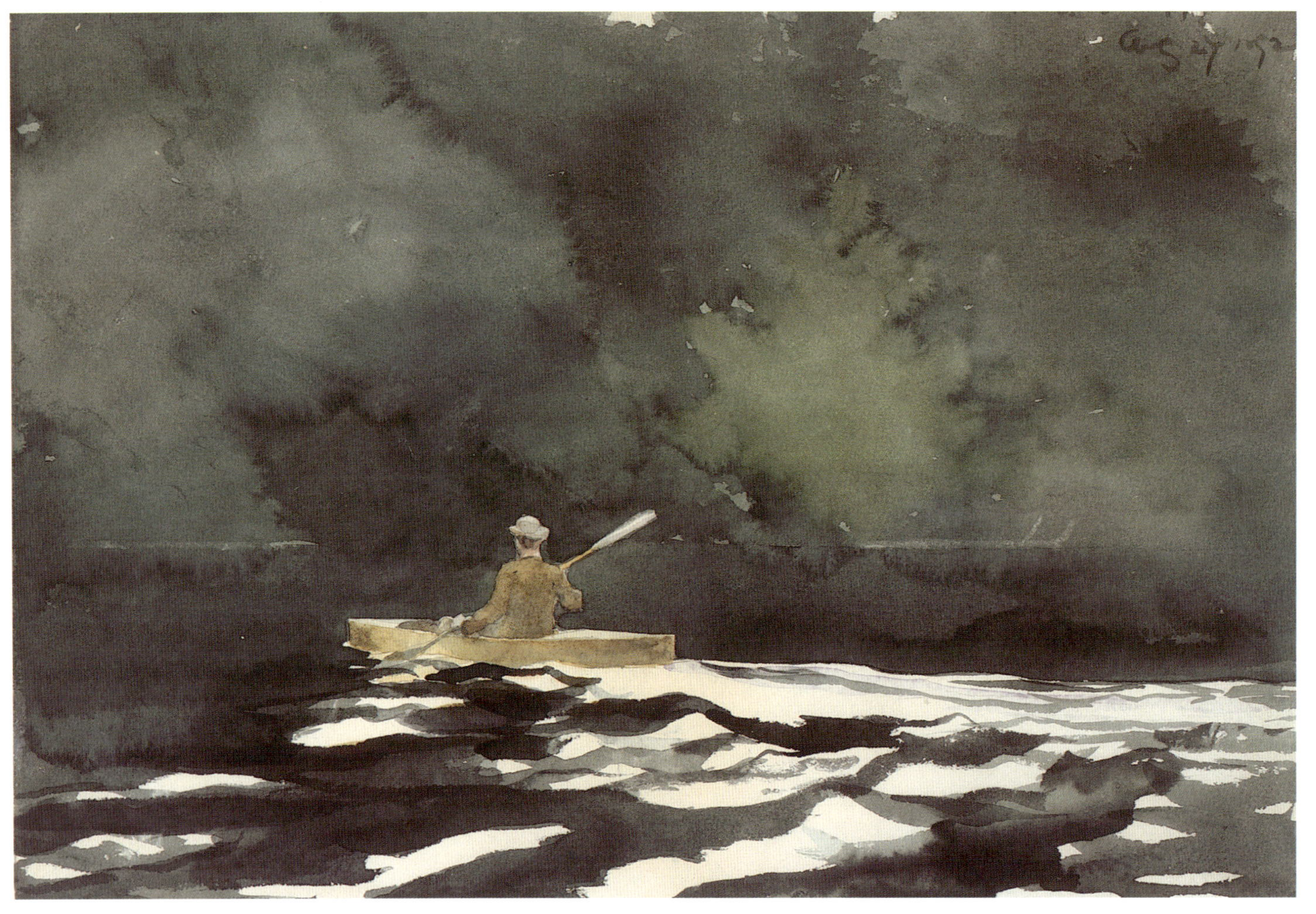

Paddling at Dusk

(1892)

Joseph Bruchac

Have you ever noticed

how many of those

in Homer's paintings

are turned away,

their backs as eloquent

as any face as they move

into the landscape?

Like the artist himself,

their eyes are their own.

Paddling at Dusk

(2000)

Joseph

Bruchac

Paddling at dusk,

perhaps not far

from the North Woods Club

in the Adirondacks,

where Mink Pond is held

in curtains of fog,

where a blue boat skims

through the pickerelweed,

where those big woods

and hard winter spaces

can make a man

and his dreams seem small.

Winslow Homer

thought blue skies

looked like the devil,

he truly hated

the straight easy lines

of horizons

that others of his time painted.

His vision had covered

the war between the brothers,

he knew the flurry

and the blur

of life was never

as easy as that.

Paddling at dusk,

but we do not know

if that man in the hat

in that one-man boat

with his paddle upraised

is Homer himself,

if he's going away

into that grey haze

or if he is finally

coming back home.

Thomas Eakins

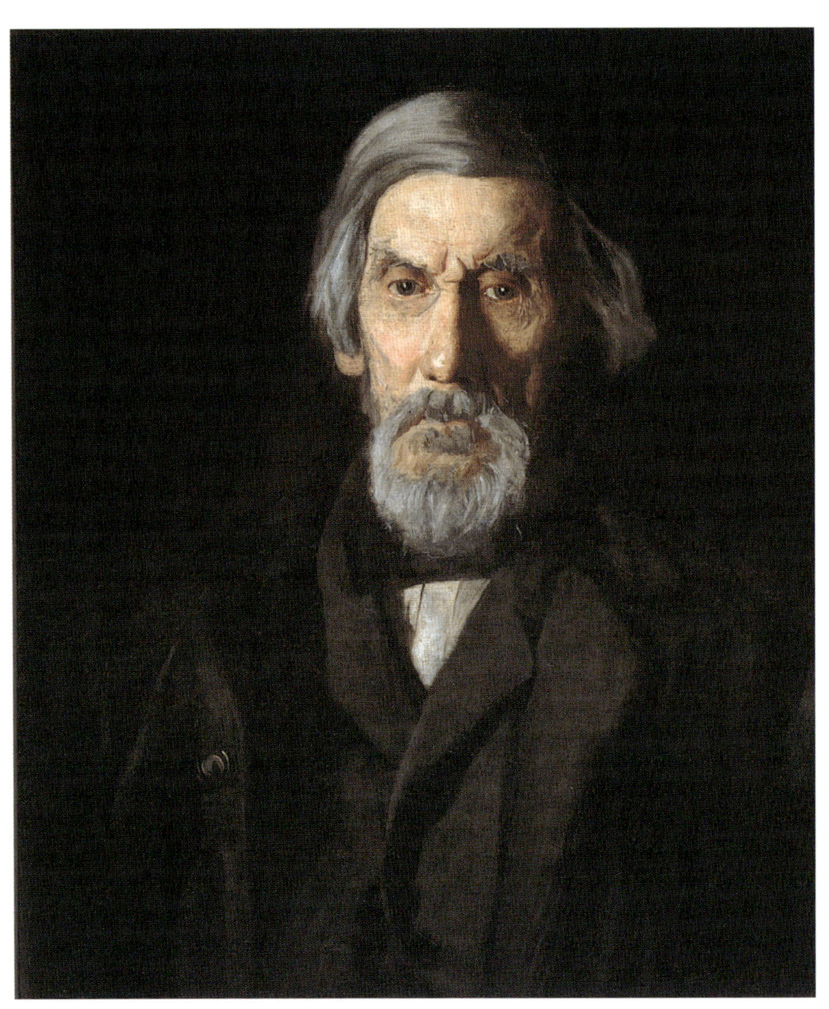

William H. Macdowell

(1904)

Hayden Carruth

Mr. Macdowell was a friend of my grandfather.

Sometimes I wonder if I knew him when I

was a boy or if I only heard about him or dreamt

about him. He said to me, "Son, everything

you see is real, and almost everything is wrong.

Remember the difference." And I always have.

William H. Macdowell

(2000)

Claude Monet

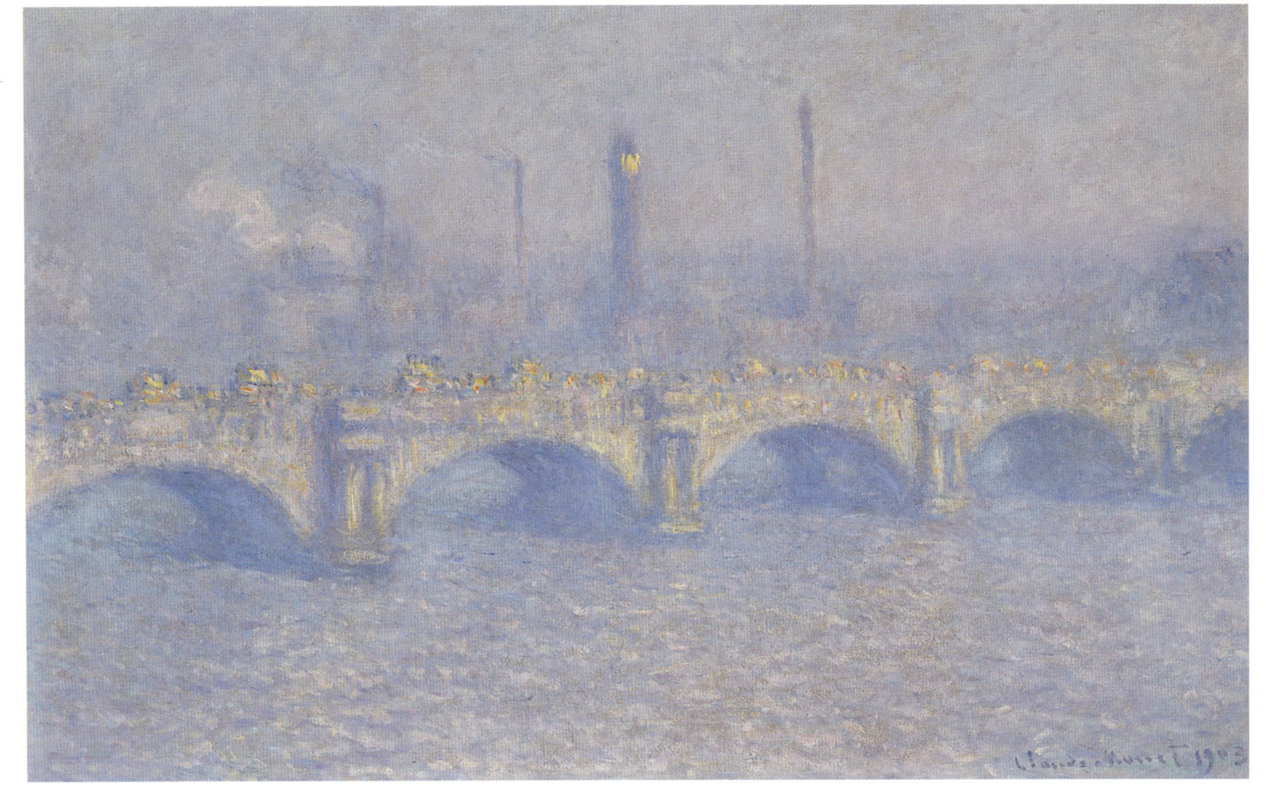

Waterloo Bridge, Veiled Sun

(1903)

Zena Collier

In 1941, George Orwell wrote that if you are English and grow up in England, the suet puddings and red pillar-boxes enter into your soul. To the puddings and pillar-boxes (England's mailboxes) I would add a third feature: the fog that was peculiar to London, my native city. "Was" because it no longer exists.

Since Monet was only a visitor to England and presumably had a Gallic palate, it's fairly safe to assume that he wasn't greatly enthusiastic about suet puddings. But fog was another matter.

"I adore London," Monet proclaimed. "And above all what I love is the fog."

Random Memories Evoked by Monet's *Waterloo Bridge*
(2000)

For this painter of light, fog was a subject to be captured and recorded. He was obsessed with its ephemeral quality, its ever-shifting form and hue, the atmosphere it conferred on Waterloo Bridge and other London landmarks he painted.

For Londoners, however, the fog was quite another cup of tea. For them, the dense, swirling, yellowish-grey miasma know as peasoup fog—so thick that it made you cough, so acrid that it stung your eyes and throat, so dirty that it rimmed your fingernails in black and deposited grime on collars and cuffs—was a seasonal nuisance to be taken for granted and stoically accepted as an integral part of winter.

For a child growing up in London, however, the fog was a source of wonder and delight, though not for reasons of artistic inspiration. I was fascinated by the way even the most familiar sights became other-worldly, mysterious, and slightly—thrillingly—menacing when blanketed by fog. I marvelled at the way people in the fog became wraith-like or totally invisible. I loved it when fog hushed the sounds of voices and footsteps in the streets, and slowed the city's tempo as traffic proceeded at a crawl or was forced to stop entirely. I especially liked the way the dimly seen outlines of double-decker buses became ghostly pachyderms as their drivers inched them along, or finally brought them to a halt for fear of hitting someone or something in the billowing murk. In this event, the bus conductor, whose job it normally was to stand on the boarding platform taking fares and dispensing tickets, would jump off the platform and walk carefully along the street in front of the bus, guiding the driver, who brought the bus slowly along in his wake.

Did Monet ever see that, I wonder?

Did he ever stand on Waterloo Bridge on a foggy day, listening to the plaintive sound of foghorns while boats and barges sat invisible and immobile on the Thames?

In the early nineteen forties, when England was at war with Germany and Hitler's Luftwaffe nightly attacked London, a thick fog was always welcome. "A bad night for the bombers," people said with satisfaction. Far preferable to a clear night with a bomber's moon illuminating targets, shining down on the river by which enemy pilots charted their route to the city.

"*Old Father Thames keeps rolling along, Down to the mighty sea*," we sang at school back then.

"Louder, girls!" the music mistress ordered. "Put your hearts into it!"

"*Miiiighty seeeea*!" we trilled at top volume, affirming the eternal verity of the river, endlessly flowing despite the worst Hitler could do.

The fog is no more. (Do I hear a faint *hélas*?) It began with the Industrial Revolution of the nineteenth century when factories burned coal as fuel. Over time it diminished as other cleaner fuels came into use, and by the middle of the twentieth century it was gone, even before the Clean Air Act of 1956 took effect.

Gone, too, is the Waterloo Bridge that Monet painted, the nine-arched bridge designed by John Rennie that opened on June 18, 1817, the second anniversary of the Battle of Waterloo. That bridge was replaced in 1945 by a graceful five-arched bridge designed by G. G. Scott. Like its predecessor, the later bridge offers fine vistas and is an ideal place from which to observe how London curves around the river.

But it was the earlier bridge that occupied a special place in my heart. Not, I must confess, because it was painted by Monet, but because of a perfectly dreadful Hollywood movie, *Waterloo Bridge*, which I saw in 1940. I was fourteen, and England had been at war for a year. And as I sat, entranced, in the velvet darkness of the cinema, watching handsome Robert Taylor, as an English army officer, first encounter beautiful Vivien Leigh, as a would-be ballet dancer, on Waterloo Bridge during a World War 1 air-raid, a real-life World War 2 air-raid was in progress outside the theatre, the *crump-crump* of anti-aircraft guns providing an accompaniment to what was happening on-screen.

Engrossed in the heartbreaking love story, I hardly noticed. I grieved for the lovers' separation as Robert Taylor departed for the trenches. I was devastated by the unspeakable fate of Vivien Leigh who, through a plot line that only Hollywood could have devised, was subsequently reduced to earning her living as a member of the Oldest Profession, though never for an instant did she lose her air of refinement as she plied her sordid trade on—where else?—Waterloo Bridge. Or rather, on a Hollywood recreation of Waterloo Bridge.

Several years later, shortly before the end of the war, I got engaged. My engagement party was held at the Savoy Hotel, which even after nearly six years of wartime austerity, was still elegant. I wish I had known then that, forty-something years earlier, Monet had stood on the balcony outside his fifth-floor room at the Savoy, overlooking the Thames, painting Waterloo Bridge enshrouded by fog. Painting it over and over again as the light changed and the fog shifted…

Decades later, long after I'd moved to America, and England and youth were far behind me, I developed cataracts, for which I had surgery. Next day, when the operated eye was uncovered, I was astonished and delighted as vivid colour flooded my vision. Could the leaves on those trees I saw through the window really be that brilliant green? Could that Mediterranean-looking sky of azure blue actually be the dull, muddy Rochester sky I'd been seeing for years?

I thought then of Monet, diagnosed with cataracts in 1922, at the age of seventy-two, many years after his Waterloo Bridge series. For some time his paintings had been growing muddier, fuzzier, with fewer details, and the colours had taken on a yellowish-brown tinge. Unlike me, however, Monet had become aware that something was affecting his vision.

"I no longer painted light with the same accuracy," he told a reporter. "Reds appeared muddy to me, pinks insipid, and the intermediate or lower tones escaped me."

The blues especially had gone down, which is typical of the condition.

After cataract surgery, Monet's ability to see colours, particularly blues, returned sharply. With the fog, so to speak, removed from his vision, he finally completed his late-life waterlily cycle, in which the blues and lavenders glow as softly and truly as they do in his 1903 rendering of the bridge veiled by fog in the vibrant city.

Edouard Vuillard

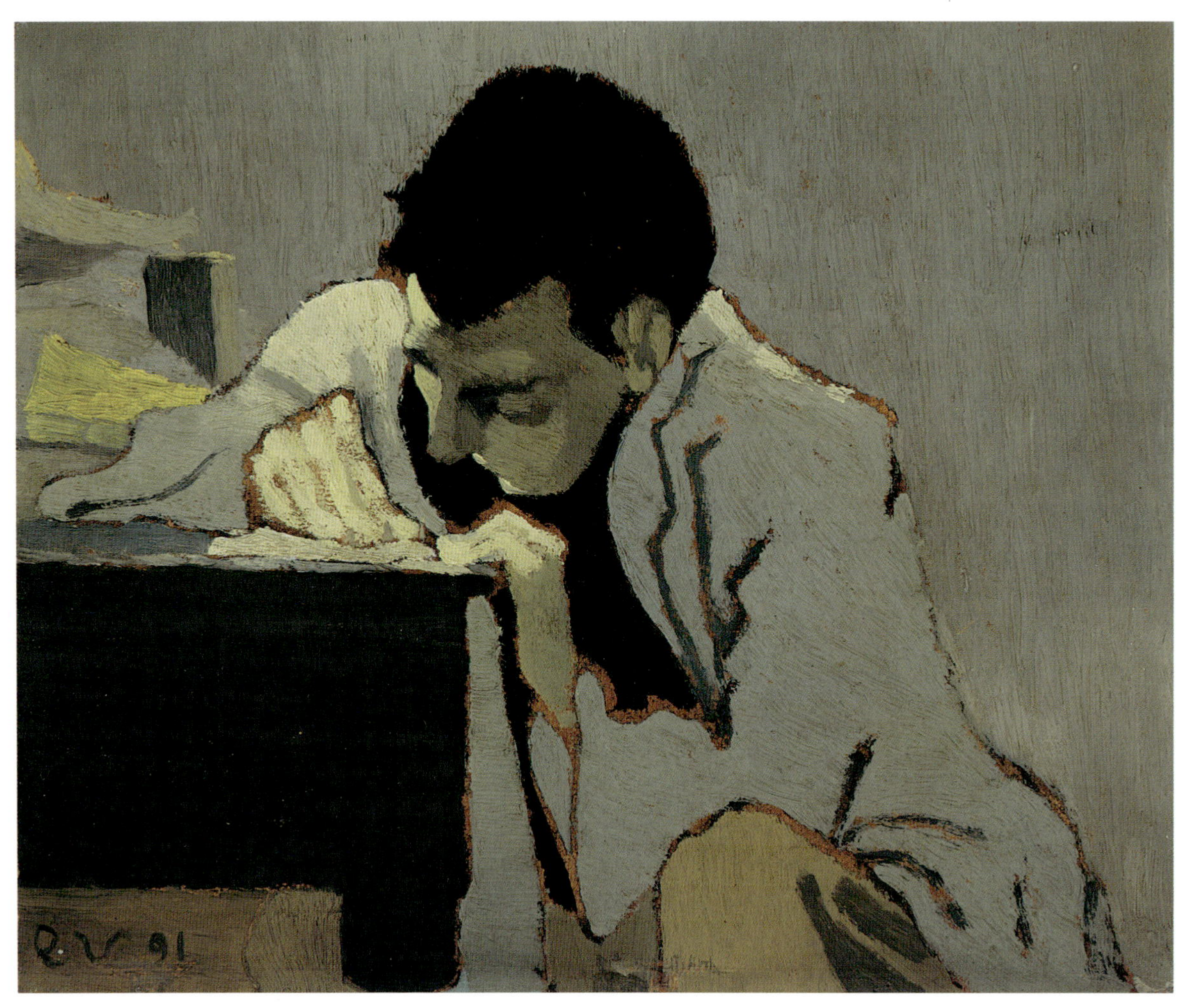

Portrait of Lugné Poë

(1891)

Robert Creeley

As if a feeling, come from nought,

Suspended time in fascinated concentration,

So that all the world therein became

Of that necessity its own reward —

I lifted to mind a piece

Of bright blue air and then another.

Then clouds in fluffy substance floated by.

Below I felt a lake of azure waited.

I cried, *Here,* here *I am — the only place I'll ever be …*

Whether it made a common sense or found a world,

Years flood their gate, the company dispersed.

This person still is me.

As If

(2000)

Jacob Lawrence

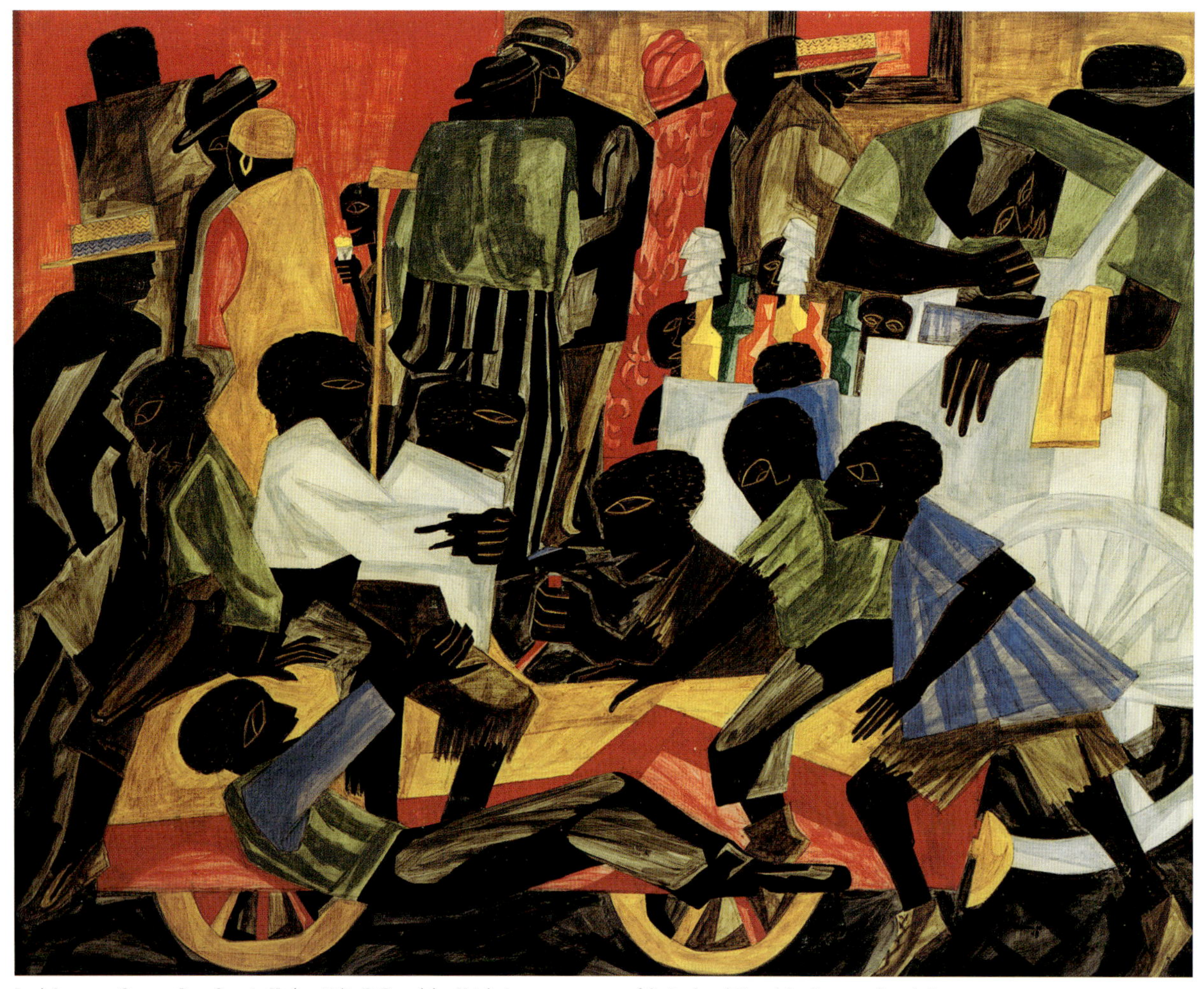

Jacob Lawrence, *Summer Street Scene in Harlem*, 1948. © Gwendolyn Knight Lawrence, courtesy of the Jacob and Gwendolyn Lawrence Foundation.

Summer Street Scene in Harlem

(1948)

Cornelius Eady

You don't see the sun, but you know it's around.

You can't smell the sweat, but it stains the canvas.

You can't enter the buildings, but you've felt the

Hot walls clamp your blood.

It's simple; heat rises.

It's easy; sleeves roll up.

Nothing to it; the stoop is

Everyone's living room.

Jacob Lawrence: Summer Street Scene

(2000)

You can't hear a word, but your ear's

Drunk from stories.

You'll never be introduced,

But you've met their landlord.

It's elementary; asphalt radiates.

It's a snap; ice sweats a glass.

This is how the first shift ends,

Plain as dirt.

July's jazz, August's hot bop.

You can't ask their business, but you know

How they'll rise the next morning,

Their groggy, heat-tossed steps

Back to work;

Sleepwalkers through the temporary cool.

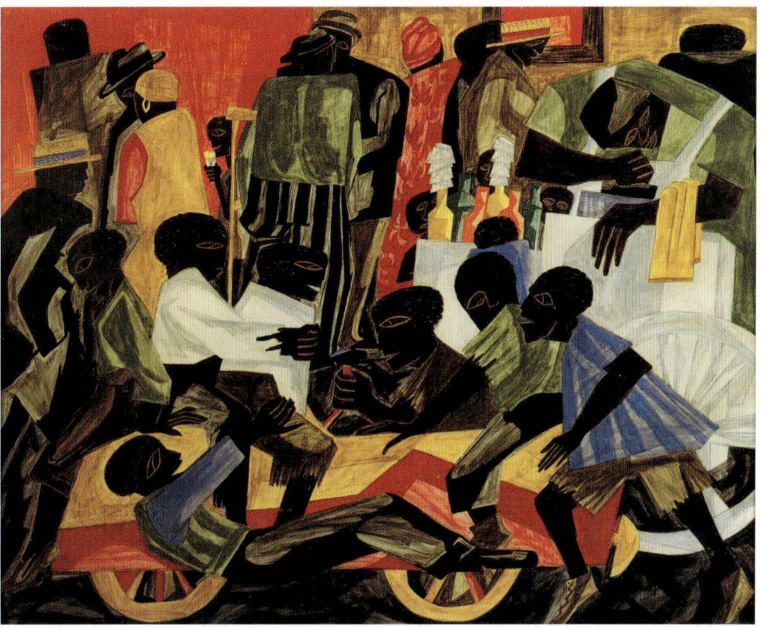

Jacob Lawrence, *Summer Street Scene in Harlem*, 1948.
© Gwendolyn Knight Lawrence, courtesy of the Jacob and Gwendolyn Lawrence Foundation.

Winslow Homer

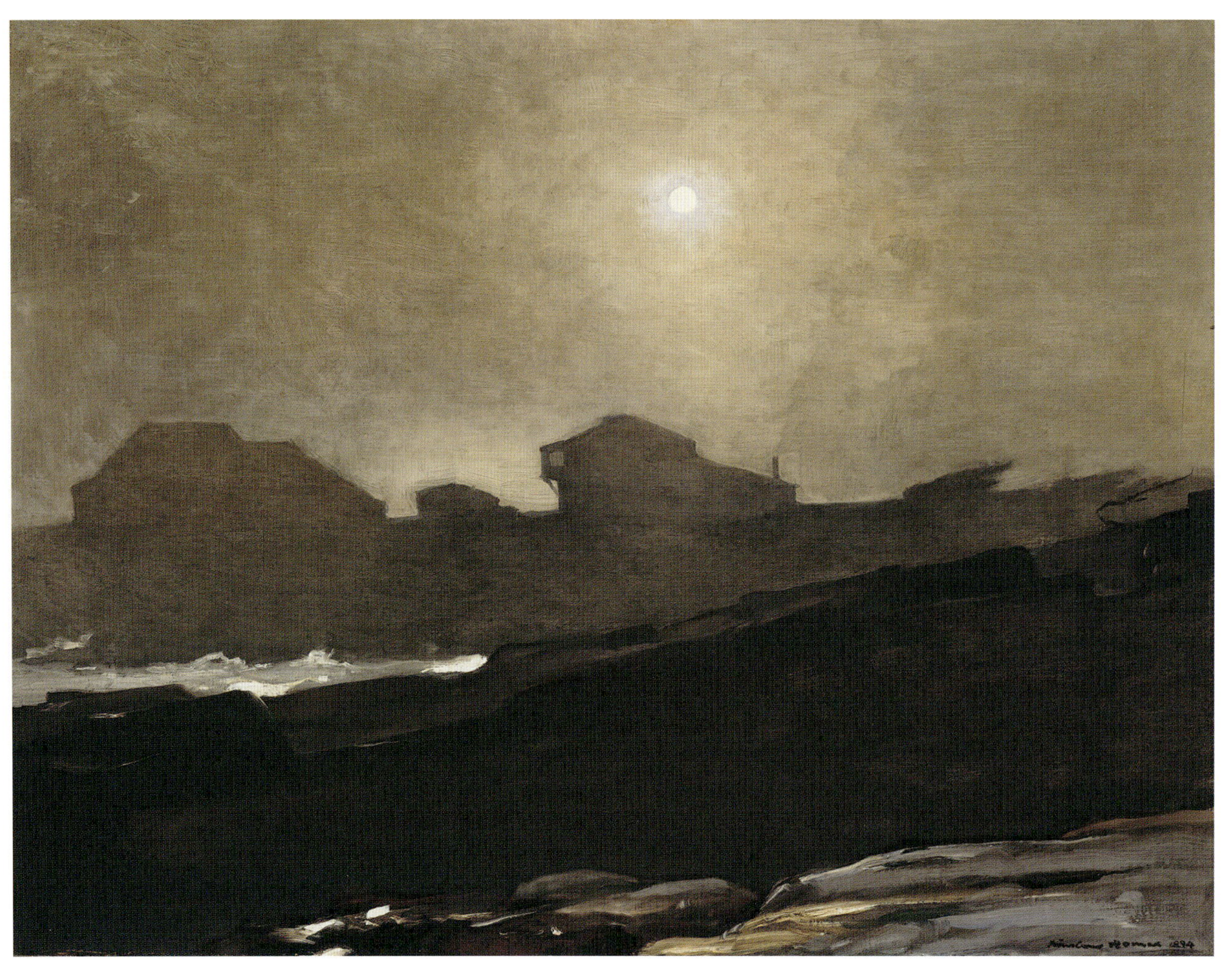

The Artist's Studio in an Afternoon Fog

(1894)

Thomas Gavin

He is in no mood for trusting mirrors. At dinner with Mattie and Charles—a silver cream pitcher. A pear-headed man on its belly mocks his every gesture. When his hand creeps toward the pitcher, the pear-head's fingers fatten. He wants cream for his coffee, but his dwarf-twin glares from the pitcher, daring him to reach. He holds his wrist to the table edge, his hand like a mouse caught by the tail. "What is it, dear? Shall I get the bismuth?" When he reaches, a hand on the pitcher looms to meet his, bloating from the pear-head's sleeve. He grips the handle, *will* not tremble as he pours. Then, careless how liquid sneaks to its lip, he tilts the pitcher to his face, and the pear-head's brow balloons. The bulbous eye glancing away from his glance is furtive, blurred. Impossible to know.

Self-Portrait: Prout's Neck

(2000)

Later that day he confronts his shaving glass. The head-on gaze he knows is false, but he thinks:

If I catch him unaware.... He angles a hand mirror to frame his profile. No good. The hand

holding the mirror gives him away.

That night, undressing for bed after a restless day peering from his gallery at a pelting storm,

his hand freezes above a collar stud. On the black window glass a strange man tries, moment by

moment, to hold himself still, to disappear into the invisible pounding of waves.

Next morning he wakes to the foghorn baying across the cove. Collects his easel, a canvas and

paints, drops an apple in his pocket and leaves, inching the door to its jamb. Slinks from his

home like a burglar. Gulls squeak above. Waves thump the rock. He stalks across the cliffs,

away from all mirrors, fleeing the grotesque selves that haunt them.

Nothing tempts his eye.

All day, nothing. He turns, at last, to go back. And catches his breath.

There in the fog: not his brother's house and his own, anchored in rock—but their silhouettes.

The rock a long swell, the Ark of Charlie's house riding its crest, and in its wake his own tight

craft, wrapped in a yellow-gray roil, the brow of his gallery jutting, under a sun whose stare he

can return.

There on the slippery ledge, gulls wheeling above, alive to the bustle and thud of the sea, he

planted his easel and mixed his oils. Distance and fog, the medium of vision.

Francesco Ubertini

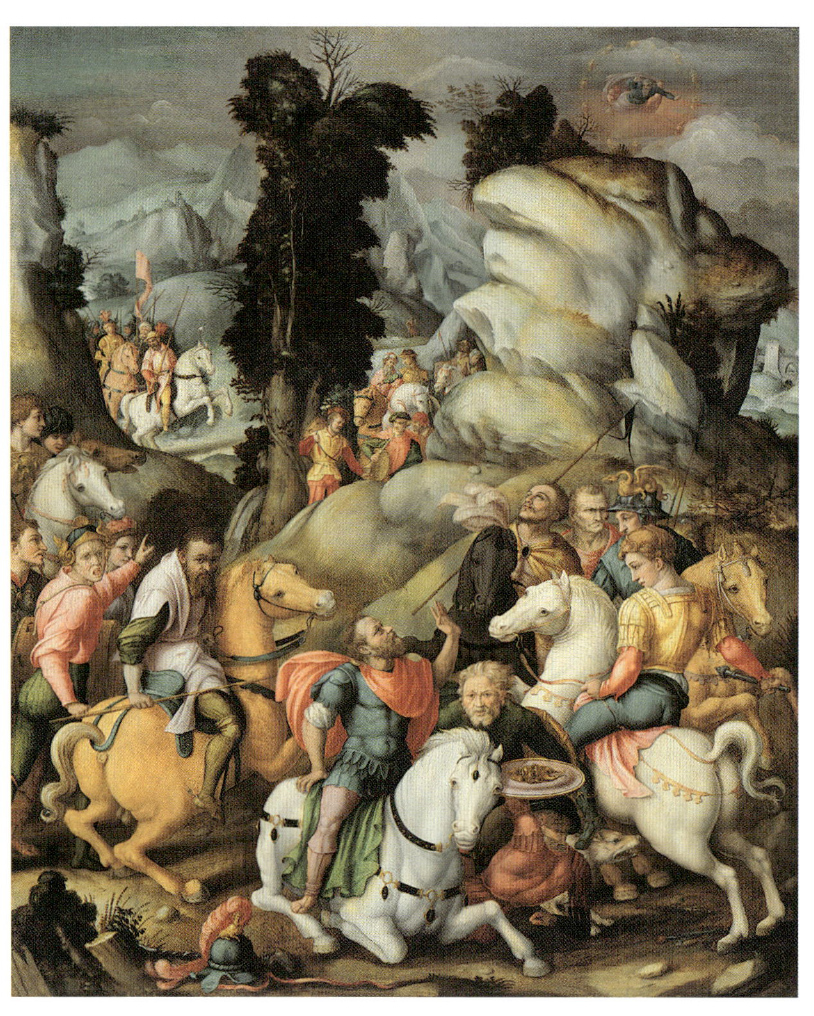

The Conversion of St. Paul

Anthony Hecht

What happened? At first there were strange, confused accounts.

This man, said one, who had long for righteousness' sake

Delivered unto the death both men and women

In his zeal for the Lord, had tumbled from his mount,

Felled by an unheard Word and worded omen.

Another claimed his horse shied at a snake.

Yet a third, that he was convulsed by the onslaught

Of the falling sickness, whose victims we were urged

To spit upon as protection and in disgust.

Rigid in body now as in doctrine, caught

In a seizure known but to few, he lay in the dust,

Of all his fiercest resolves stunningly purged.

The Road to Damascus

(2000)

We are told by certain learned doctors that those

Thus stricken are granted an inkling of that state

Where *There Shall Be No More Time*, as it is said;

As though from some pail spilled water were to repose

Midair in pebbles of clarity, all its weight

Turned light, in a glittering, loose, but stopped cascade.

The Damascene culprits now could rest untroubled,

Their delinquencies no longer the concern

Of this fallen, converted Pharisee. He rather

From sighted blindness to blind sight went hobbled

And was led forth to a house where he could turn

His wrath from one recusancy to another.

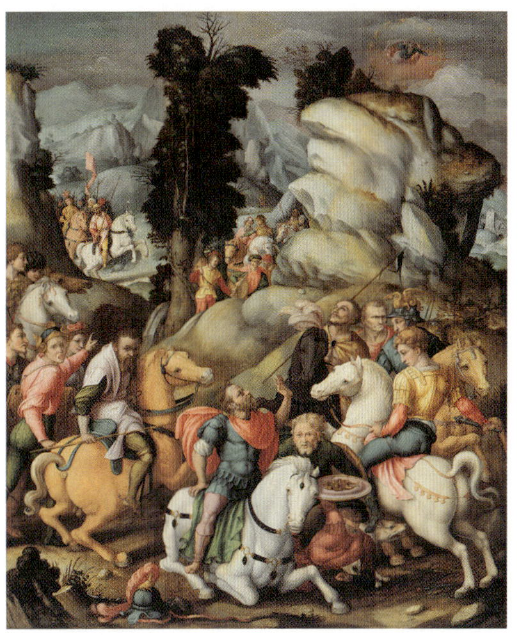

George Catlin

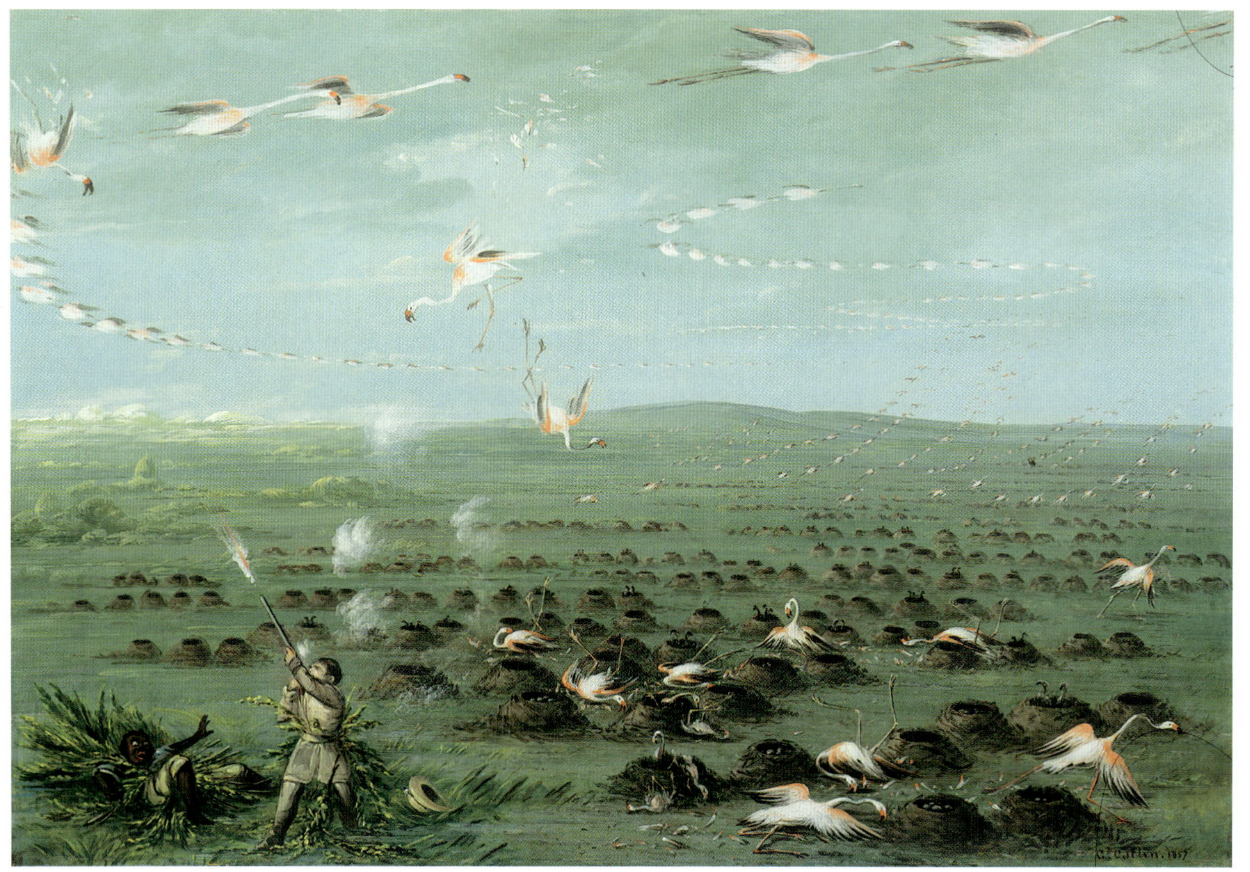

Shooting Flamingoes

(1857)

William Heyen

Catlin is sixty. Slogs to get to the place of this painting—South America, Argentina,

south of Buenos Aires. Quaking hummocks, suckholes. "Up to our waistbands in the

mud and slime," he remembers. To paint pink and pinkish-red flamingos calligraphically

aswirl or, shot, plunging into that dark: the birds becoming retinal after-images we

won't forget when we close our eyes to this dreamscape, the painting from now on

part of our unconscious in the reds and pinks and deft touches of gray-black and

white over the saline marshes.

Blam, the Colt rifle—Catlin painted this on commission from his friend Samuel Colt

to show the use of these firearms in exotic settings—having done its work, no, *doing*

Catlin's Flamingos

(2000)

its work in present tense here in the everything-at-onceness of our viewing. Birdshriek panic, a scene for us as of a momentary revelation of the undermind, all still but in motion, a foreboding here (one he can't quite reconcile in his composition). We must join him in his diversion, the high slapstick hilarity of the lower left corner.

But we must not misread or make too much of this. Laughter in George as he paints, yes, but not a bone or fleck of derision: this is the artist who sacrificed himself to honor the vanishing native inhabitants of the Americas, whose credo was, in part, "I love the people who have always made me welcome to the best they had. I love a people who worship God without a Bible.... I love a people who don't live for the love of money." And as to the effect of his profuse gallery of Native Americans, we'll keep in mind this outburst by Daniel Webster: "My God, Catlin, you have shamed me. I was blind to all this red majesty and beauty and mystery that we are trampling down."

The Negro-Indian guide, his hat and body camouflaged by grasses, has been accidentally struck by the Colt's breech as Catlin fired his first round. He's frightened out of his wits, thinks he's been shot (Catlin tells us), thinks he'll be shot again. But enough cartoonish frivolity. The painter paints himself facing away from us and his painting's subject proper, as, perhaps, he'd like not to face it. We might follow his line of fire to the particular flamingo he's hit, the one just making it into our sight, then out into skeins of birds, to two or three near ones that are falling—by Catlin's accounting he shot about a dozen this morning—to a scattering of feathers, to lower center where we sink into blasted creatures in disarray within and below the ranked fluid geometries of their nests. Here in the dead foreground Catlin has caught his own oily—how oily the green is here—and irrational and shadowy desecration of nature.

No, this painting is not of course a sermon, or an allegory, but it does brood the romantic which in its heart cherishes the natural sublime. The painter painting knows that no necessary or good thing was done here. We notice the spindly fragilities of the birds' legs, eggs in several nests, baby birds in many others. "Nests with eggs and nests with young," George tells us in his *Last Rambles Amongst the Indians of the Rocky Mountains and the Andes* as he recalls this event ten years after experiencing and painting it—the Civil War intervening with the blood of tens of thousands staining the pond at Shiloh and with the inhuman transactions of Andersonville—"the very young heads up and gaping, the older young, but without wings, pitched out of the nests or sprawling and trying to fly or to hide themselves on the ground. We replaced the little chicks in their nests as well as we could about us and left them."

Something had struck Catlin here to the depths of his being, something he couldn't quite surround: "Of all the curious hunting or other scenes I have ever seen on earth," he writes, "that scene was the most curious." Trying to apprehend what is happening here in the painter, what word or words would we substitute for the deflections of "curious"?

No, it was not a good thing that was done here in wild nature this morning, nor can a painting (or the several he did on this subject) escape this act or redeem it. And he, the preserver and rememberer of what was being lost, was this time responsible for what we won't forget as the beautiful flame of his nineteenth-century flamingos fuses with muck and death in our souls.

Kathleen Cunningham McEnery

84

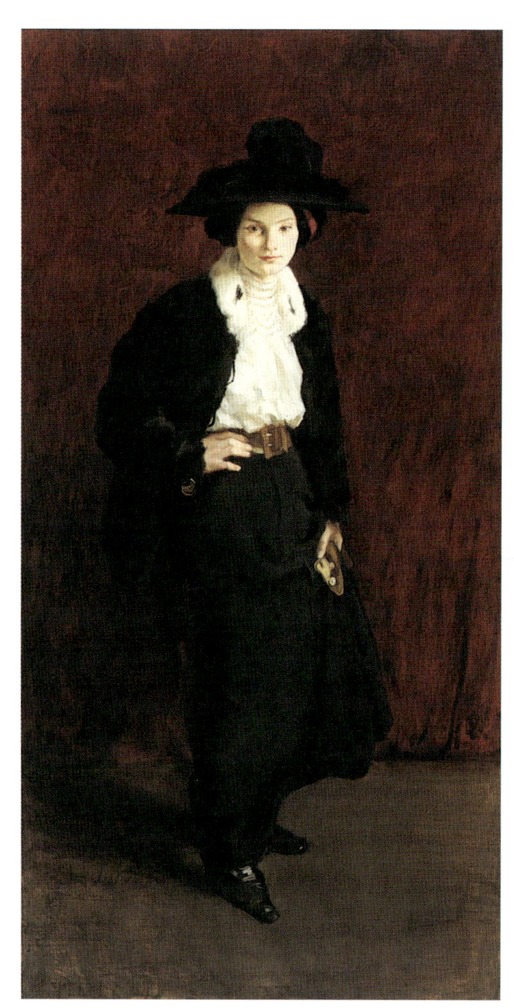

Woman in an Ermine Collar

(1909)

Susan Holahan

A sharp-featured, russet-haired young woman, bundled in black, her hat suave as a coal sack

dropped on a board. Does she almost fail to emerge from her setting? Light makes a panel,

a kind of icon, of her face, her collar, her blouse—all creamy. Her hands gleam below like

unconsidered jewelry.

Is this The New Woman? The year is right. Her eyes look new. But these clothes with their

folds and gathers keep her steps small. Her shoes won't last one city block. And no one chains

herself to a fence for Women's Suffrage or suffers force-feeding in jail in an ermine collar.

If not The New Woman, then The Gibson Girl? But the Gibson Girl was dressed and painted

to be looked at. This one here's looking at you, kid. Her near hand on her hip, her hip cocked

at an angle to knock your eye out. No titled Lady propped against furnishings, pets, children,

Woman in an Ermine Collar

(2000)

Susan

Holahan

this woman has nothing but her outfit and her attitude to face you with. Though

you will never hear her name, she's prepared to face you down.

A woman in an ermine collar does her looking freely, faces out boldly.

Ermine, after all: royalty wore it, once. But whose ermine collar is it, anyway?

In 1908, an American woman—born in Brooklyn, now twenty-three, single,

studying painting in Spain—wrote to her family that her teacher found her *too*

clever. Go home, he said. DEVELOP YOURSELF!

Did she ever take advice? She headed for Paris, where the neo-

Impressionist paintings in the Salon made her laugh. Then they made her angry.

She knew she could do better.

The next year, she found an ermine collar to fit a foxy model's face,

her style. The model—had she worked for Rodin once? then quarreled with the

fierce, famous sculptor?—was happy enough to pose for a young American.

Posing paid the bills.

The Young Woman's bold gaze belongs to the painter, who thought well of

herself and why not. She was smart. She had talent to burn. She'd try almost

anything. Though she never traveled without an older cousin as a chaperon,

she seemed to know what she wanted. The sharp eyes above the ermine collar

show us how she saw herself in her salad days.

Soon she was painting in New York City. Her name was made forever by two canvases submitted to a show jury in 1913. Not small, not pale, not timid; two sizable, challenging oil paintings, a total of three NAKED women. They hung at the Armory alongside the work of men who became Famous American Painters. She never turned into a Famous American Painter, but no one who met her ever forgot this was The Young Woman Who Had Two Nudes in the Armory Show.

In 1914 the Young Woman Who... married the Cunningham automobile (people called it the American Rolls-Royce) and moved to Rochester, N. Y., where the brand-new Memorial Art Gallery included contemporary American paintings in its founding collection.

She bore and raised three children. She ran a large house on South Goodman, where she had architects add a loggia and a studio. She helped found the Harley School. She enjoyed The Corner Club. She supported women's suffrage. She tossed the salad formally, formidably, at the table. She required bright conversation.

If she wore ermine herself or voted regularly once she could vote legally, no one who knew her in Rochester—and didn't everyone in Rochester know her?—thought to mention it.

She may have painted, from time to time, after breakfast.

Leonard Wells Volk

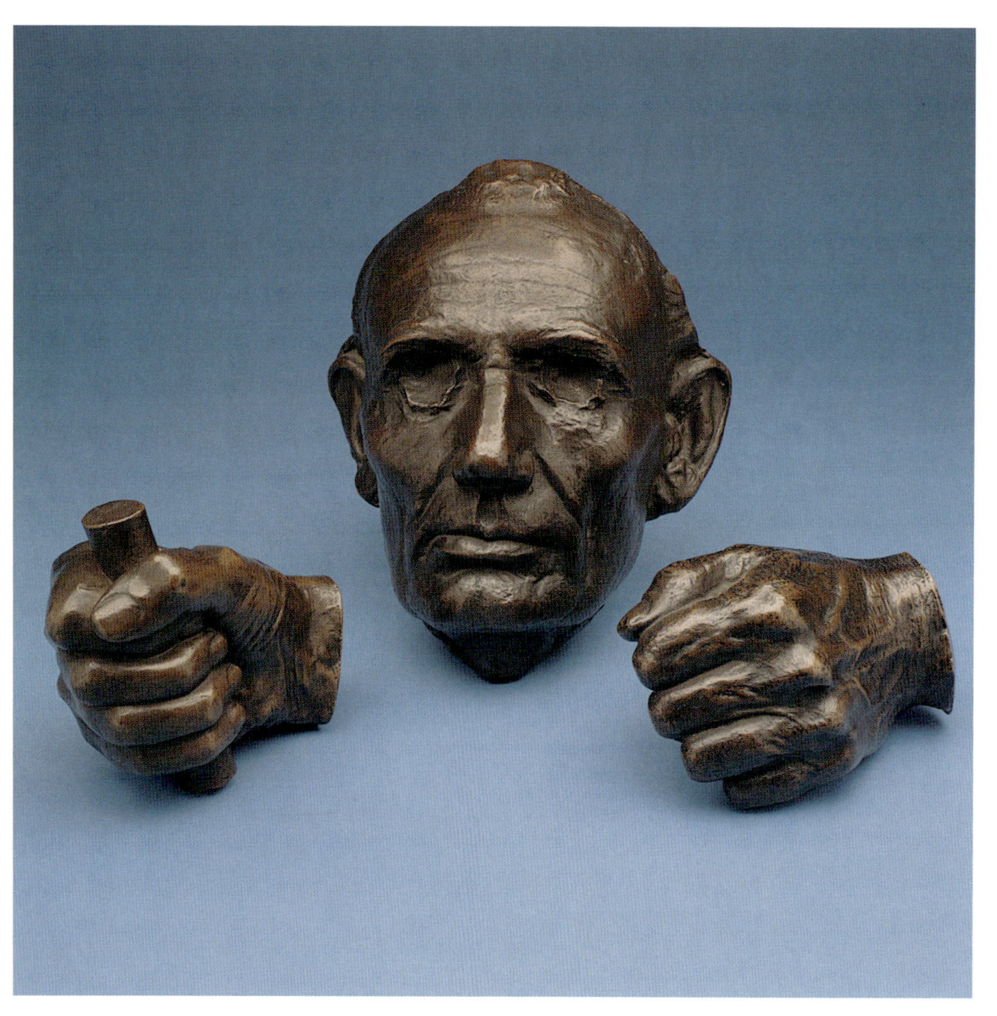

Life Mask and Hands of Abraham Lincoln

(1860)

Ben Howard

Cast in bronze and silent under glass,
    they keep their peace amidst
the landscapes, the chat of passers-by.
    The left lies flat, as on
a letter; the fingers of the right
    curl around a handle.
How delicate but how decisive
    those sculpted fingers look,
as if they held, in lasting balance,
    the mollifying touch
and, when warranted, the will to strike
    or sever. *I now wish*
to make the personal acknowledgement
    that you were right and I
was wrong. So he wrote to General
    Grant on July 13,
1863. As though they flowed
    within these metal veins,
his accurate phrases cross my mind,
    their courtly eloquence
and candor undiminished. Tell me
    if this is how we last,
our words no more erasable than bronze
    or faces carved in stone.

Lincoln's Hands

(2000)

Winslow Homer

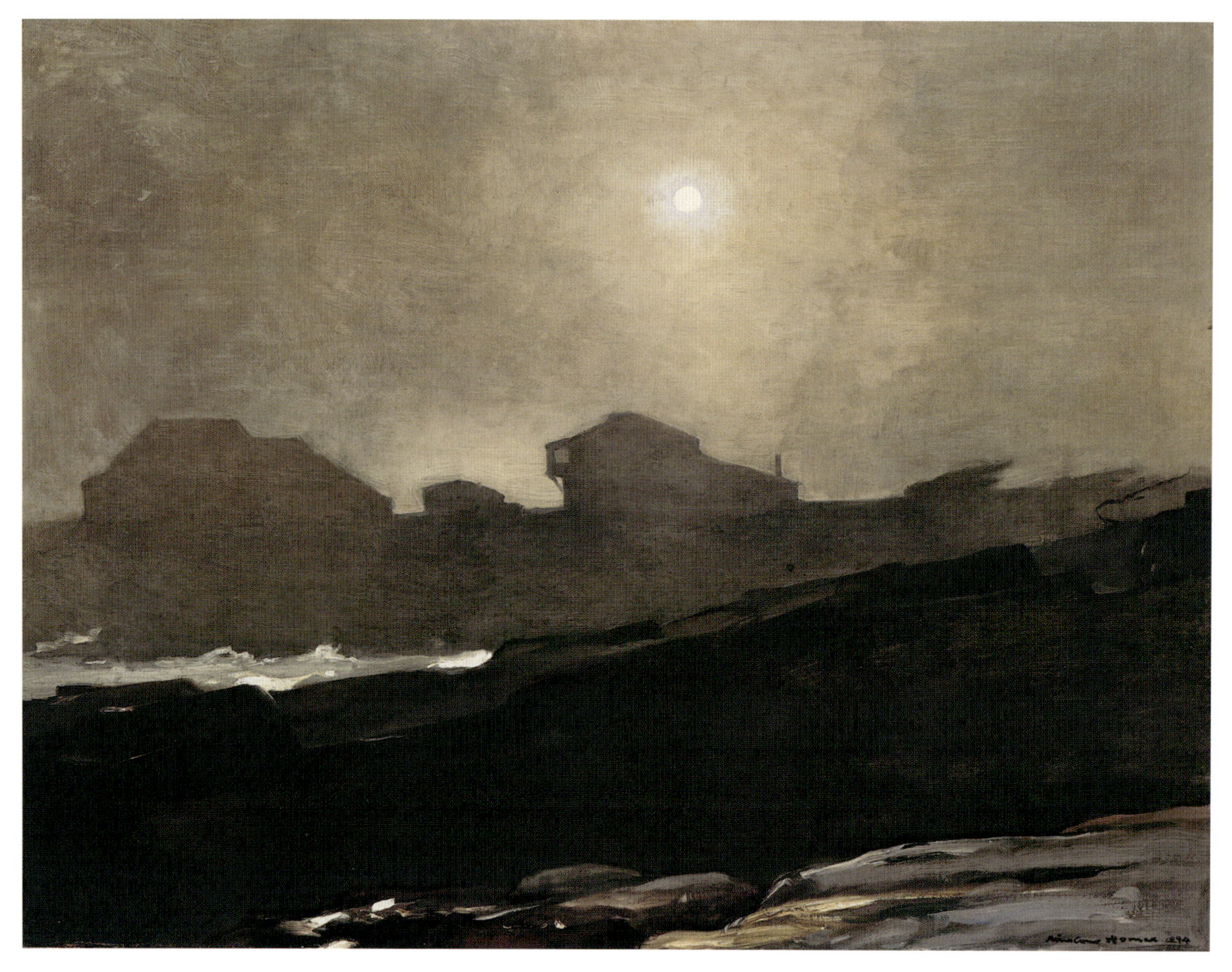

The Artist's Studio in an Afternoon Fog

(1894)

Susan Howe

All that is and all that is

Listen listen map all that

sea are you looking at sea

Goading ice wind arrowly

am I to fear the waves or

is memory cradle cradle

Whippoorwill you sing so

native to my own freely

Late afternoon fog

(2000)

Susan

Howe

To the lettered unmindful

goading ice wind arrowly

slant line who hail drift

sky so clear as something

legendary leaning where

arctic spectral moonlight

Slow sea song between that

clouds must veil something

legendary so twilight deep

homelife double backward

Atlantic to zigzag last array

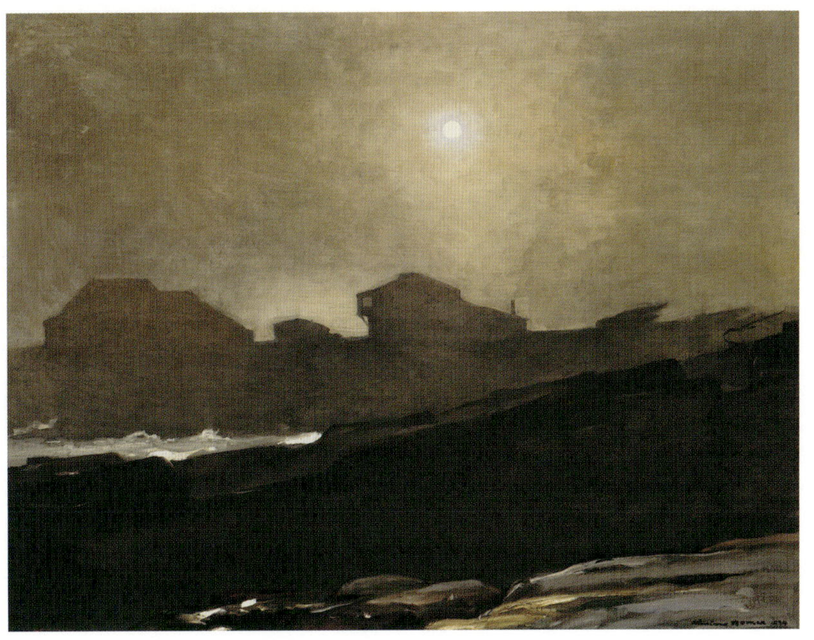

Richard LaBarre Goodwin

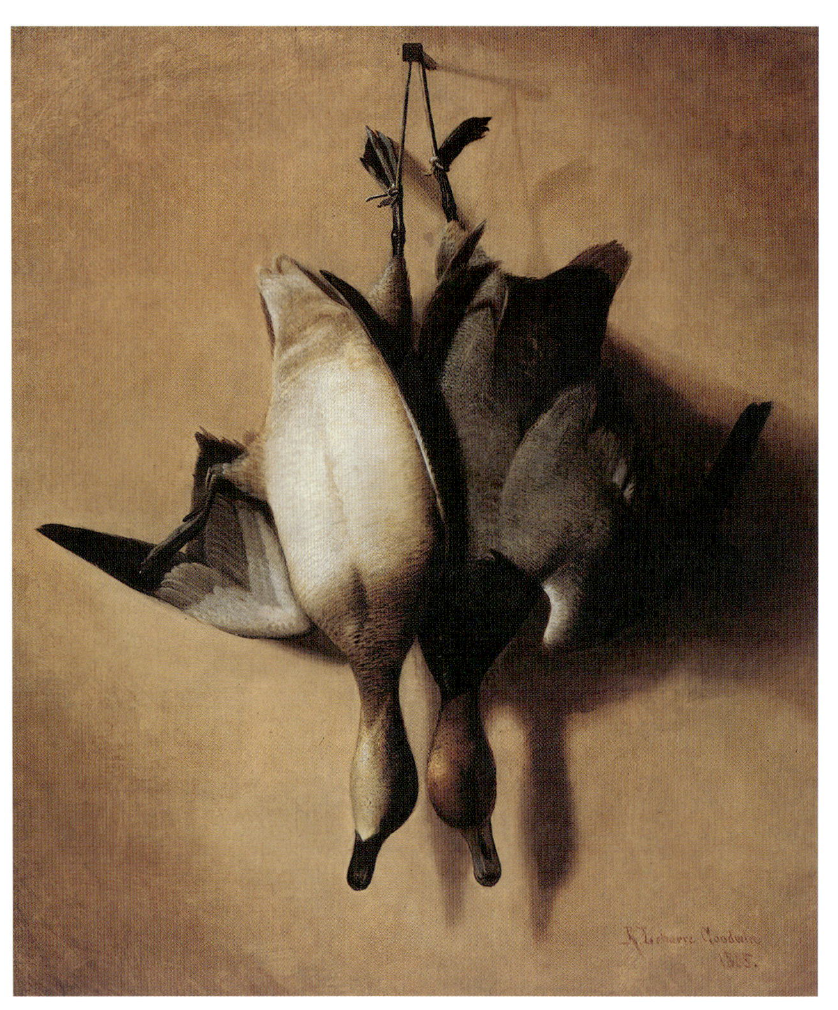

A Brace of Ducks

(1885)

Steven Huff

When I was eleven I went hunting with three other boys.

We were bad kids: we didn't have rifles, but we had

slingshots we'd made with rubber stripped from inner

tubes that fired nails like shrapnel. They were lethal. We

kept them under a stone wall in the hedgerow of a farm.

It was an afternoon after school when we went hunting.

We walked to a pond along a railroad where a dozen or

so ducks were bobbing.

A long freight train was stopped there—we couldn't see

the end of it in either direction—its shadow falling over

A Brace of Ducks

(2000)

the pond. The ducks paddled toward us, probably thinking we were going to feed them. Instead we opened fire. With four of us and pockets full of nails it seemed impossible that we missed, but we did, churning up water. The ducks lifted into the sky, quacking in panic. I wondered if any of the other boys felt as relieved as I did.

The instigator was Tim, a tow-headed boy who usually had dirt caked on his face. He blamed the rest of us for our failure to bag a duck. "Stupid shits," he called us, wrinkling his nose, and adding, "Where *were* you?" as if he had gone it alone and we hadn't fired a shot. He was inscrutable to me anyway. Tim had pictures of dead game on his bedroom wall, like a deer over the bumper of a truck, or a goose hanging from a nail in a hunter's cabin. He had cut them out of *Argosy*, or some other men's magazine. I don't know what turned him on about bloody animals hanging on his wall, but I suppose they were prizes he wanted.

I said we should hide in the trees a hundred yards off and wait for the ducks to return, though I really didn't want to do this. But Tim turned and stalked off toward the freight train, and we followed. It was getting late, the sunlight slanting red. The train felt cool when we touched its iron, as if it had just rolled out of the mountains.

Tim climbed up the ladder of a hopper car and swung himself into the open framing on the rear end of it. LaVerne climbed up and sat beside him, bracing himself with his legs like Tim did. Pete and I sat in the framing of the next car, facing them. Tim wiped muddy sweat off his face and told us more of what he thought of us. None of us could beat him up for this. All of us had tried at one time or another. Two or three of us at once, even. His father was a scab mason who moved his family into a rental house in our neighborhood to work construction on a new school building after the union went out on strike. He often put Tim to work with him, carrying concrete blocks. So, his kid muscles felt taut and hard to the touch like a drawn bow.

I knew Tim had a vein of good in him. He had trouble at school, and trouble at home where he was beaten as a matter of course. But none of that meant anything to us. I can't explain why we couldn't keep away from him. And every time we went anywhere with him we risked trouble. I began to imagine I would end up like one of his dead fowls, nailed up in justice for some stupid thing I'd done under his influence, helping him vent his anger.

What we did then I had done other times. I think the other boys had too, so I don't know why things happened as they did. The train jolted a few times and rumbled into motion. As it picked up speed I jumped off, seeing my small shadow zipping along below me like a black dog, joining me at my toes when I hit, rolling into the weeds. (Once I'd gotten hurt doing this, cut by a brandy bottle that someone had thrown along the tracks.) Peter and LaVerne leapt too. Then Tim, with a face of horror, hollered that he couldn't jump.

We ran beside the train hollering, "Jump...*jump*," as it increased speed. I thought I heard him crying, but under the clamor of the train I must have imagined it. Tim's tow-head drew farther away until it looked like something hung on the side of the train, and then disappeared as the train entered a curve. When the caboose passed us the brakeman gave us a friendly wave, and we stopped running.

We were scared, of course. We wandered toward home by way of the pond, and saw the ducks resettled peaceably on the surface. Nor did they fly off when they saw us coming. That sight jolted me. It seemed to mean that Tim was absolutely gone. And, in fact, he never came back. We never saw him again. I know this sounds ridiculous, but it's true. Where could a boy of eleven or twelve have ended up? If he'd fallen or jumped, he should have been found. Even if he'd been killed, his body should have turned up. I used to imagine a hobo had killed him and buried him in the woods.

After a few weeks his parents and the police grew tired of our mismatching denials, and left us on permanent notice of their suspicions. This was years before pictures of lost kids were printed on milk cartons—milk came in bottles then, anyway. So I didn't have to look at Tim's face glowering at me every morning at breakfast. As I grew up, Tim took up residence in that part of my brain that is a gallery of events I prefer kept dark.

Eventually his parents moved away, and we boys broke into the empty house in broad daylight. We no longer needed Tim's inspiration to do such things. In a bare room off the kitchen that we remembered as his bedroom, some of his bloody pictures still hung taped to the wall. The *Argosy* pictures. And one that was real art, I guess, "A Brace of Ducks," a reproduction. And a pair of sneakers on the floor, right were he'd left them. His mom probably told herself she'd be damned if she'd pick them up.

Fairfield Porter

100

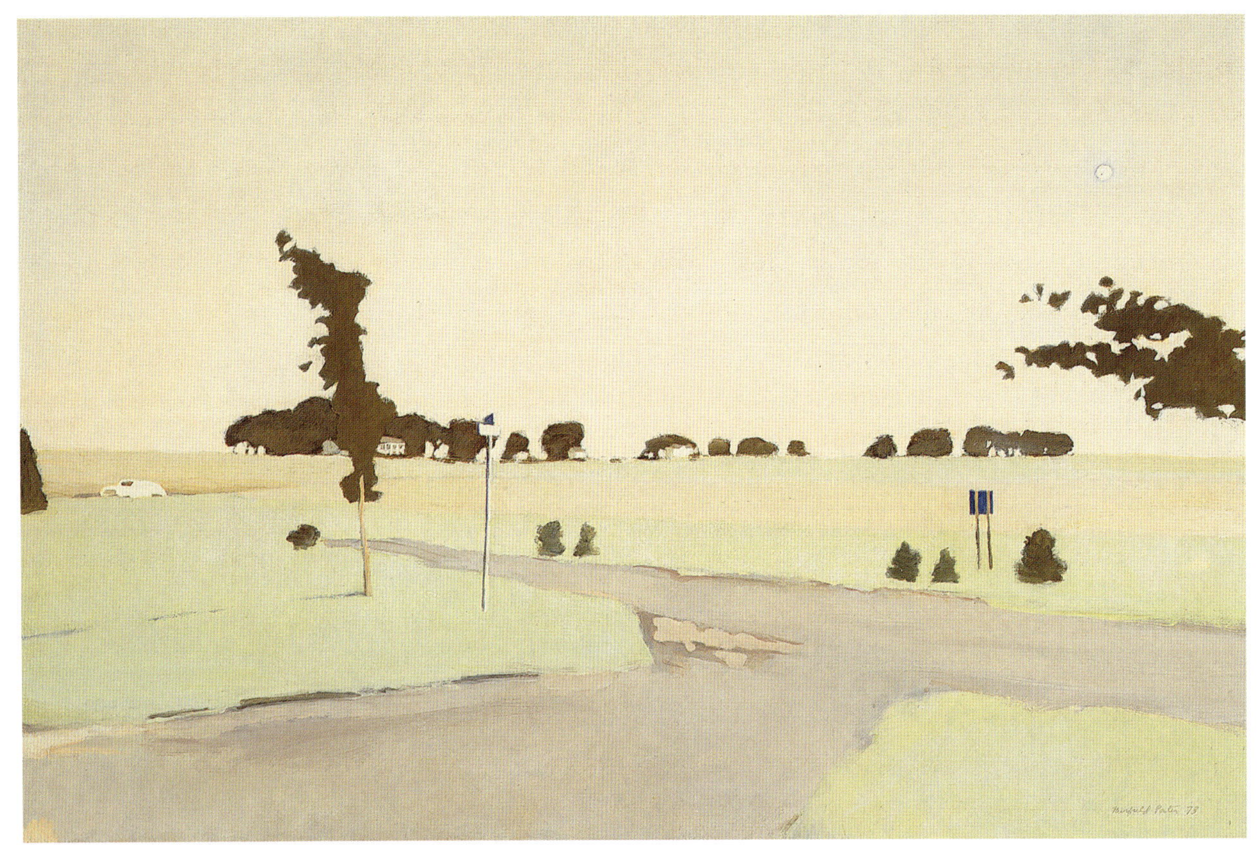

The Beginning of the Fields

(1973)

M.J. Iuppa

I know full well. I *am* getting away. No more fleeting moments.
Wishful thinking. My hands hold fast on the steering wheel's backbone.
The pressure of my open-toed shoe on the gas pedal is exact. I am getting away
in a white car on a summer road that's the color of vinegar taffy. It stretches narrowly
as it pulls around a bend, offering me another direction.

The dome of sky is melon. The midday sun strikes, unblinking.
This is an annoying dead heat. A lone poplar stands sentinel.
My car's wheels turn on whispers. I don't care.

Away is clearly a race from here to there. It's my desire to set out on my own,
without intermission, until I see that what I've dreamt at my desk, on my porch,
in the back yard isn't a mirage.

Seeing the wind-swept fields erases tension. My hands relax their grip. The tangle of
grasses surround me. Over there, in the half light, is my future.

Mother's Dream

(2000)

Roy De Forest

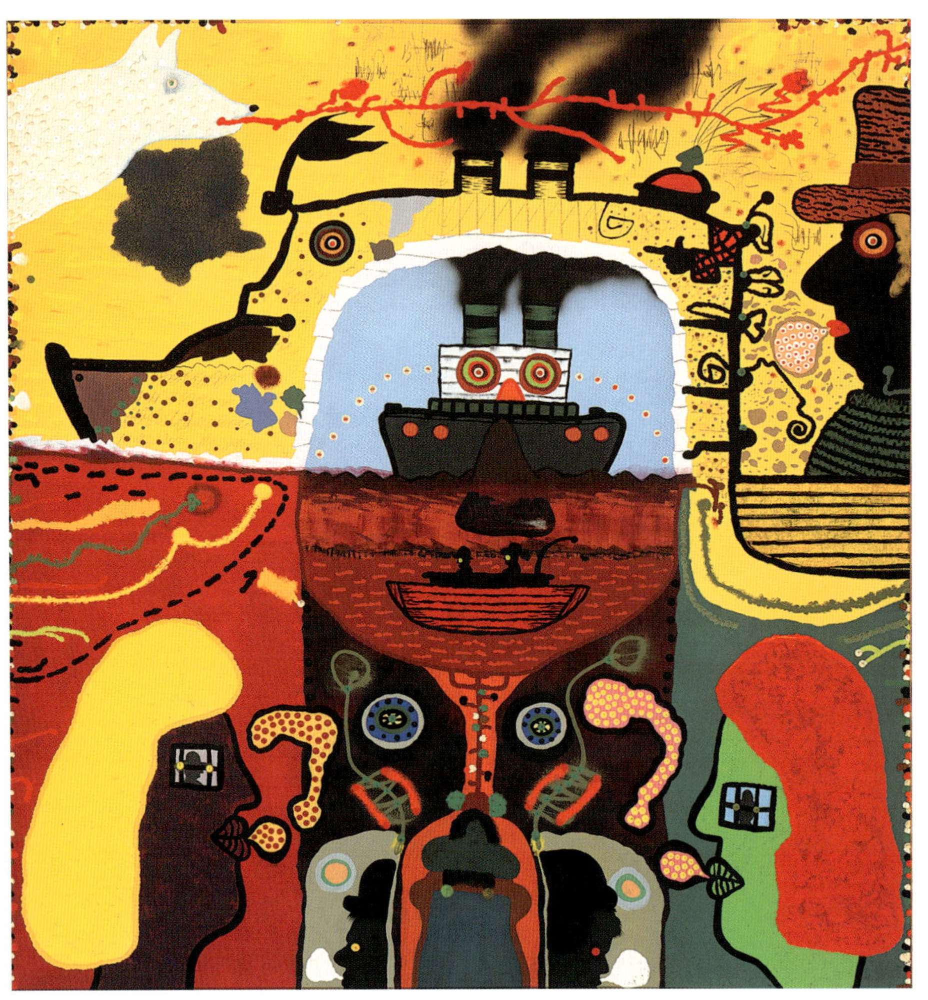

The Dipolar Girls Take a Voyage on the St. Lawrence

(1970)

Bruce A. Jacobs

Look:

I don't know

what you think you see

with that canary lantern

burning in your head.

But no way on earth there's any

bug-eyed elephant cruise liner

nosing down on our rowboat,

grinning orange as the ocean.

Next you'll be telling me

the wet sky has gone yellow

as hardened yolk, or maybe

The Jefferson Brothers Go Out for Mackerel

(2000)

Bruce A.

Jacobs

a white wolf speaks blood lightning

over our heads.

Oh, yeah, crazy weather

blowing through your skull.

Look at you, flipping your eyes

like a boated minnow,

whispering about

targets hanging in the mist,

flying saucers on clotheslines,

rockets pointed like

stern fingers.

Tell me I'm wrong, but I thought

we came here for mackerel.

And where is your rod, anyway?

What do you mean, you

dropped it?

They scared you? Who?

Two women

tall as skyscrapers

who stood in sandals on waves

and sprayed you with

cloud-spangled questions?

Yeah, I'll bet they did have

glowing jails in their eyes,

and maybe you belong

in a soft cell yourself.

You think it's funny?

I didn't row out here

to play Laurel and Hardy.

I declare,

this is the last time I'll ever

go fishing with

a painter.

Jan Davidsz. de Heem

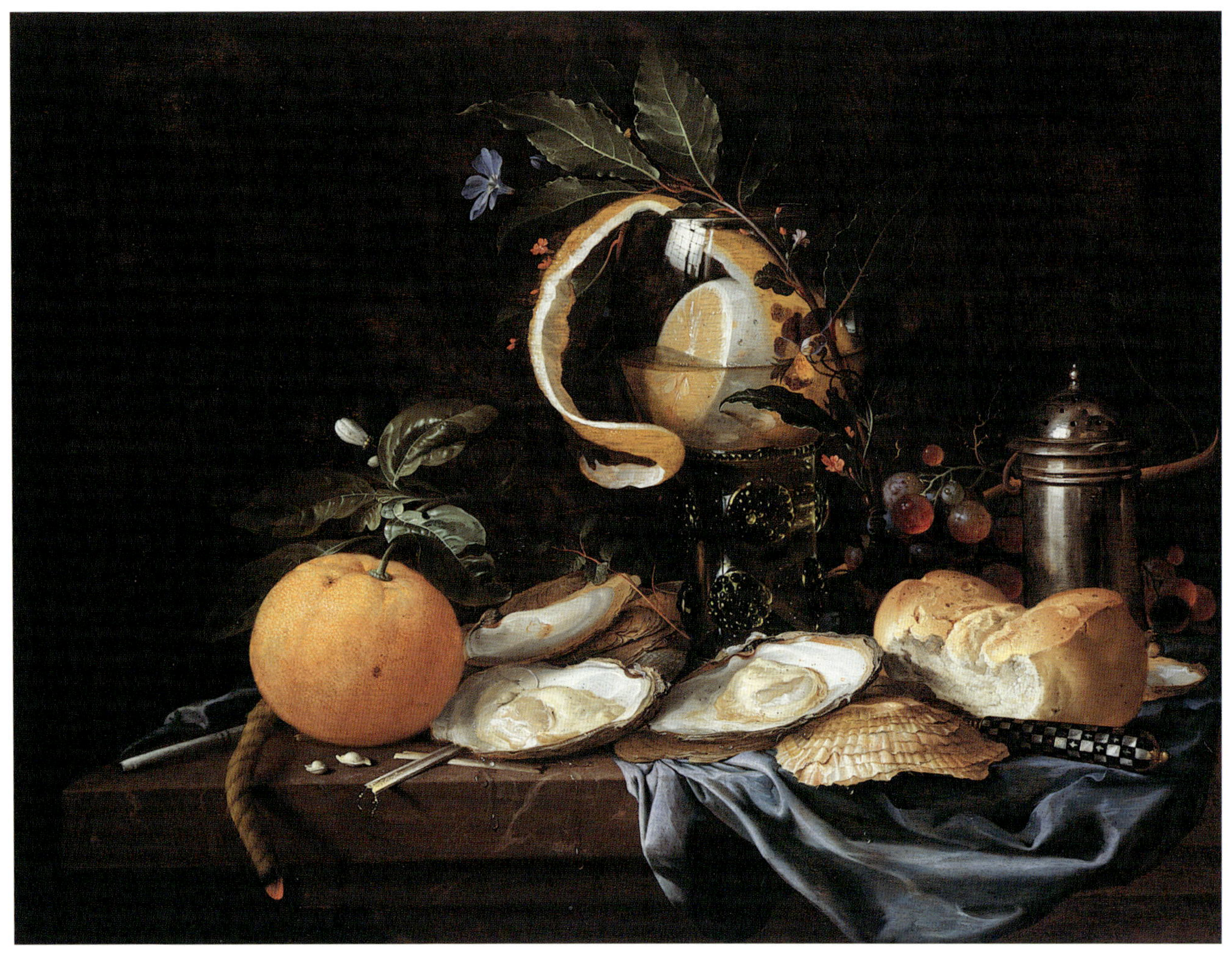

106

Still Life

(17th Century)

Barbara Jordan

How ingeniously de Heem has placed an orange

in a glass, one hemisphere submerged

to subtle distortion, and the peeled rind

unwinding like a path

we might imagine following, in miniature,

up into the air.

        In some legends

this was the fruit that Eve gave Adam —

though the apple is there too, like a tiny bomb,

its wick lit

beside shelled oysters, whose sensuousness

offers a watery flagrance

while desire grows, as is its nature,

restless.

Carnal Knowledge

(2000)

Barbara

Jordan

The glass with its grape-black stem,

embossed and palpably moist,

draws our eyes upward into the leafy shadows

of a sprig the painter's rested, somewhat coyly,

over the fruit — an enticement

out of the little world we cannot leave

without finding

if we look — just at the rim — a window

and, some say, de Heem himself at his easel

like the covering angel

                  regarding flesh and time,

how it unravels

from that twist of dangling rind —

its shape, perhaps, not unlike a serpent's?

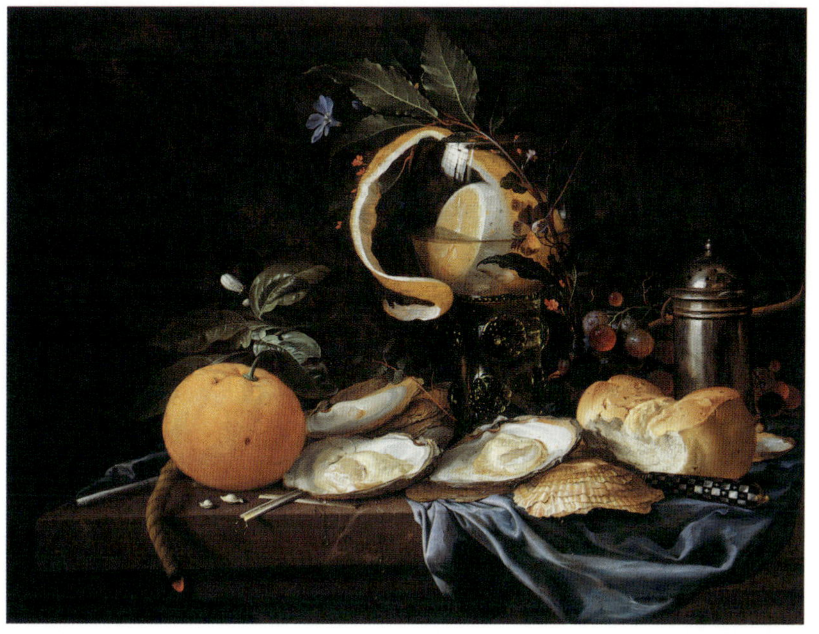

109

Charles Ephraim Burchfield

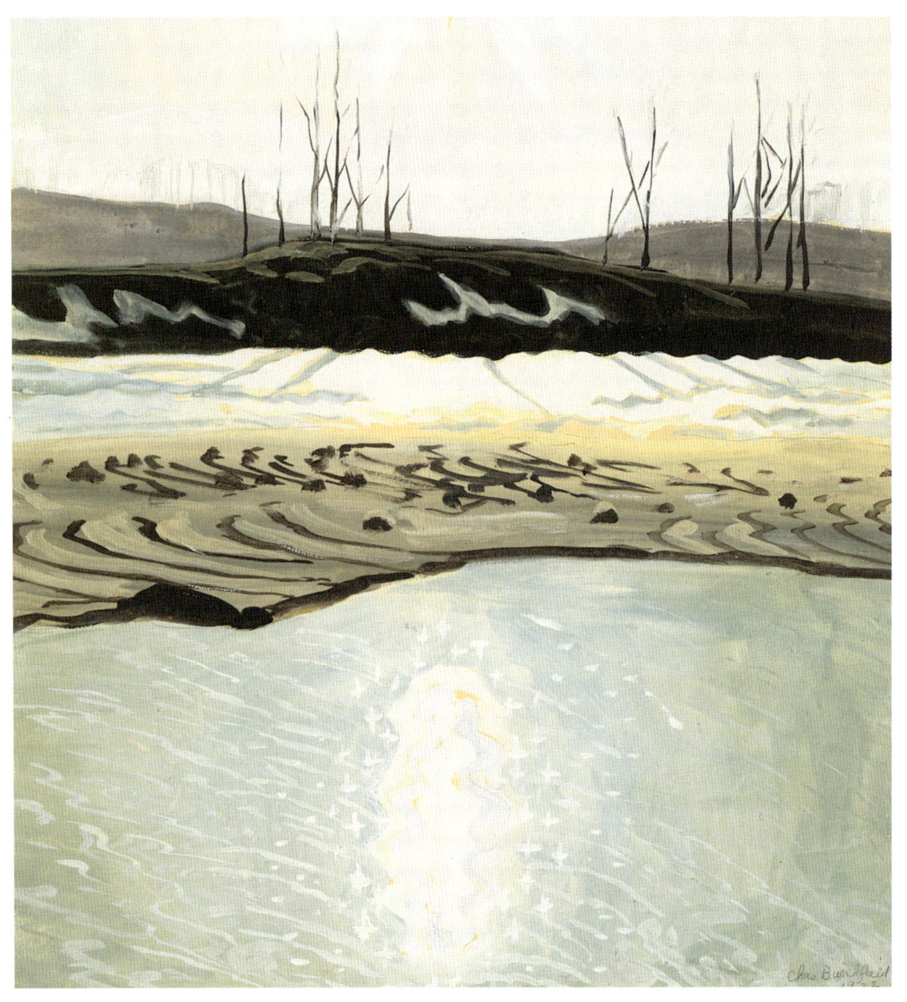

Springtime in the Pool

(1922)

Judith Kitchen

Snowmelt or rainfall in the fallow fields

fills with sky, flares an instant

in the headlights, blue. Upstate New York,

early March, where grey is absolute

and palpable. You drive through farmland—

Varysburg, Cattaraugus, Conewango.

Fields ripple with the weight

of what will be. Skeleton trees remind you

Springtime in the Pool

(2000)

what you will forget when they are full

with fullblown summer. Hint

of hidden green—green so illusory

you search for sensation, a breeze

fingering sheer gauze curtains, breeze

from before time, when childhood claimed you.

Water colored that world—sun stippled

on water, silence distended. You stood

at the edge and waited, weightless.

Green, because when you cross the Blue River

the birches that line the banks are latticed

with leaves. So light is pooled.

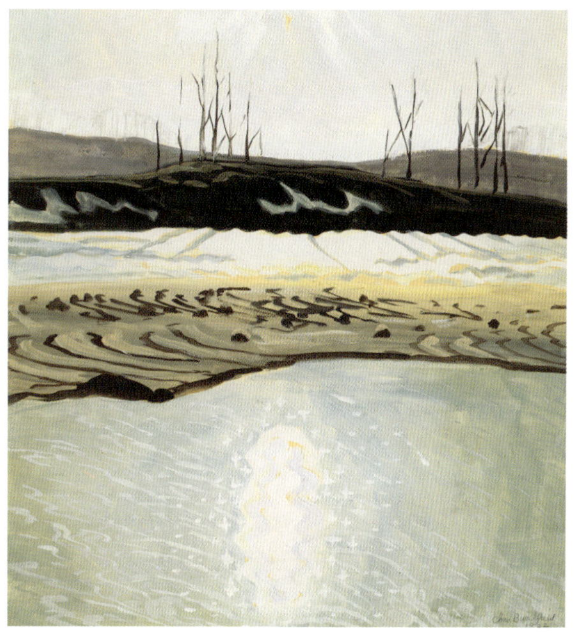

John Frederick Kensett

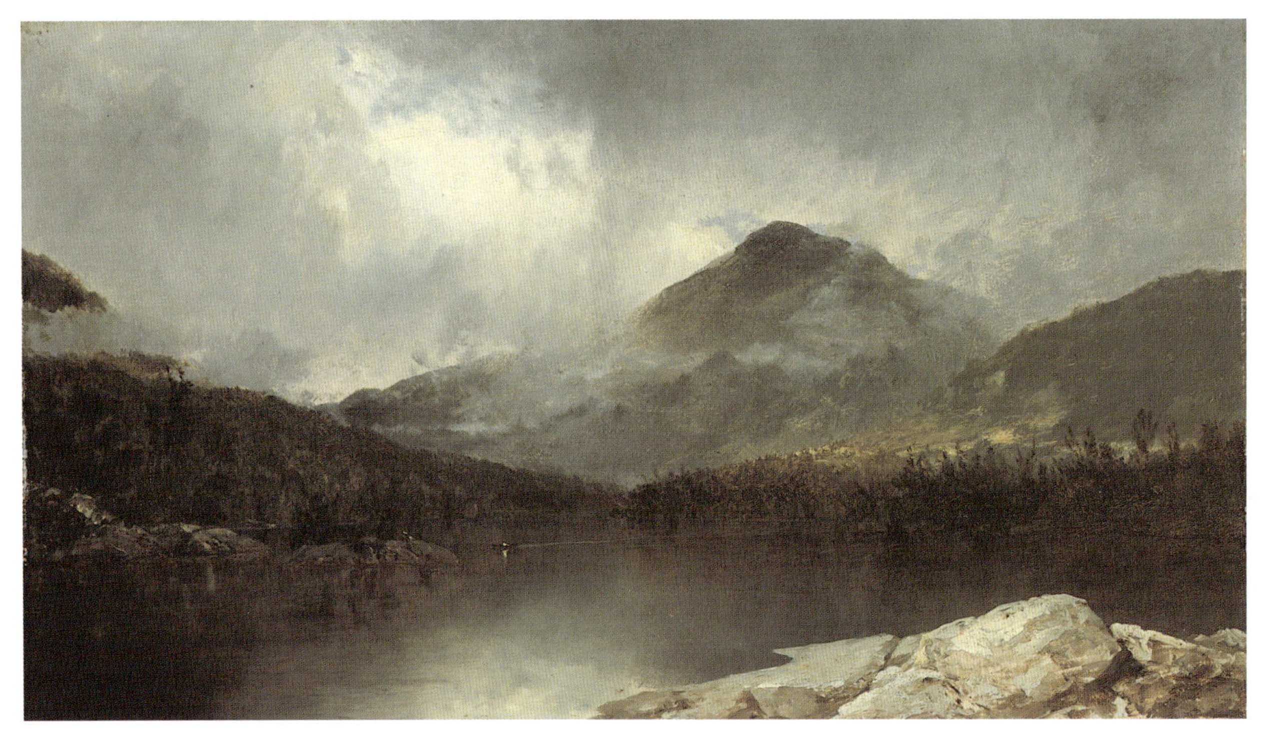

A Showery Day, Lake George

(ca. 1860)

Jim LaVilla-Havelin

Sitting on the rocks above those rocks,

soon the whole outcropping will be

slick with rain.

And I will slide and cling, tearing up

my hand on rock

to get down. Jagged rip across my hand:

blood and rain.

A Showery Day, Lake George

Jim

LaVilla-Havelin

For now, the glass of lake mirrors

      clouds, changes and breaks

      in fog piercing,

      in droplets' circles.

Silent, oars dipping through silver,

John Isaacson crosses to the cold island

      in mist:

A far worse place to be than this,

      these rocks.

For now, I am content to sit

      perched here and soaked,

watching clouds, low enough to be

      the breath of mountains

silver the day, the rocks and the water.

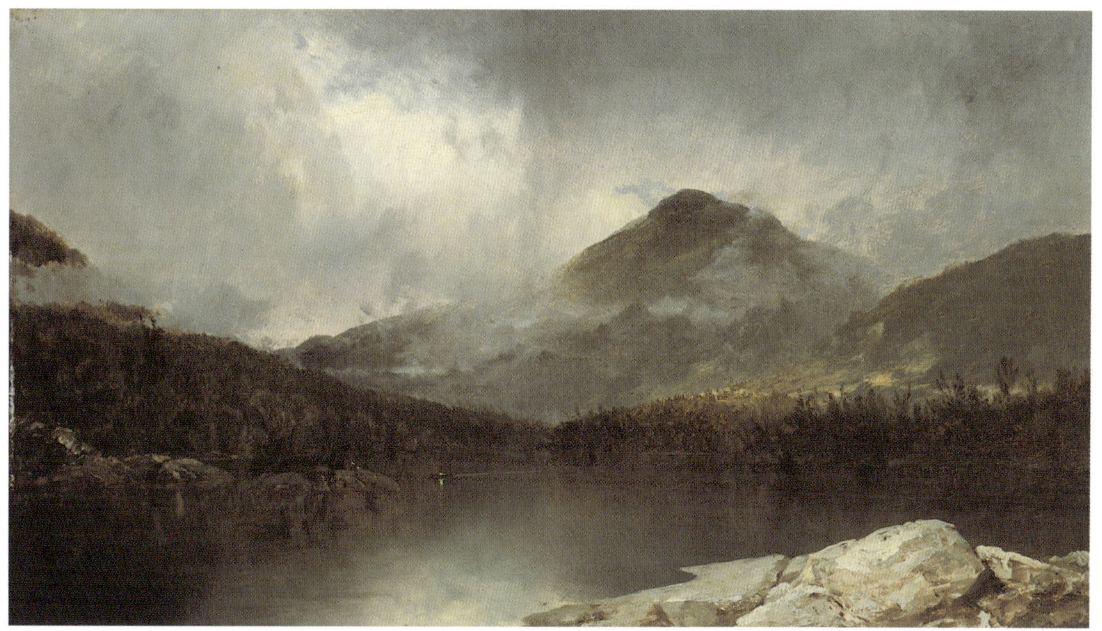

Beverly Pepper

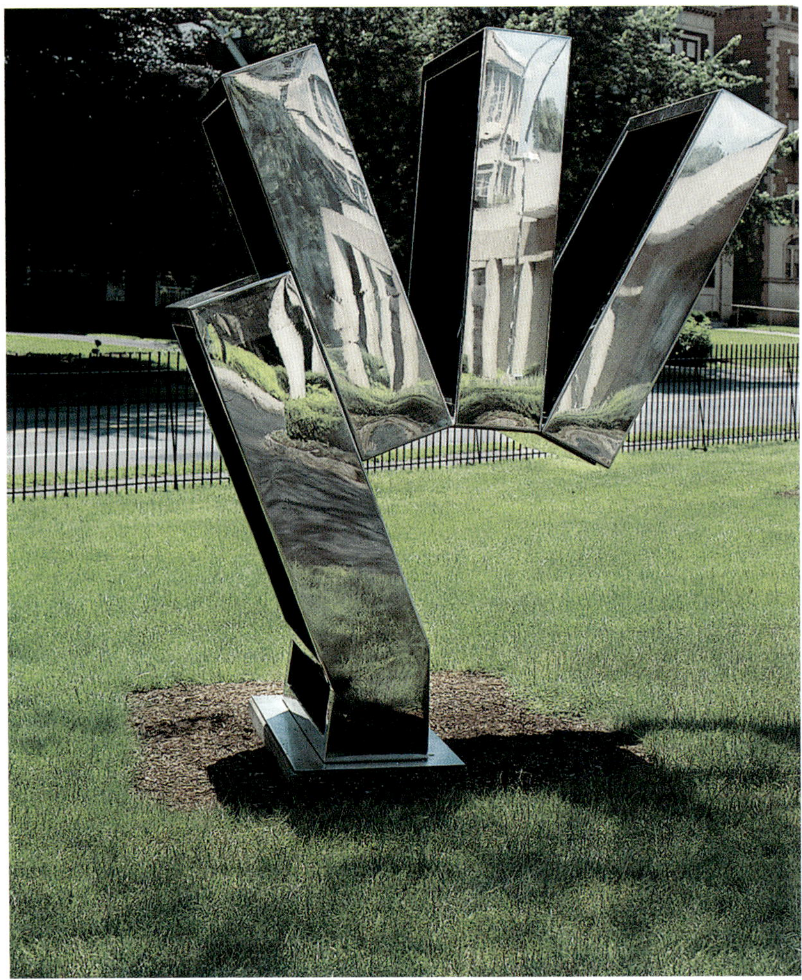

Beverly Pepper, *Vertical Ventaglio*, ca. 1967-1969. © Beverly Pepper/Licensed by VAGA, New York, NY/Marlborough Gallery, NY.

Vertical Ventaglio

(ca. 1967-1969)

James Longenbach

Someone asked me if I knew you

> *I am an object falling through space*
>
> *The reflection of sky in itself*
>
> *A heft*
>
> *I am nothing to hide*
>
> *Inside I am bluer than sky*

I didn't know what to say

> *When you look at me the void seems filled*
>
> *Solids empty*
>
> *The reflection of your face*
>
> *These lines*
>
> *At certain times of day I am invisible*

But I do like to look at you

> *An object of sky in itself*
>
> *The inside solid*
>
> *Your face these*
>
> *Lines each morning when you look at me*
>
> *You disappear*

Lines

(2000)

Anonymous

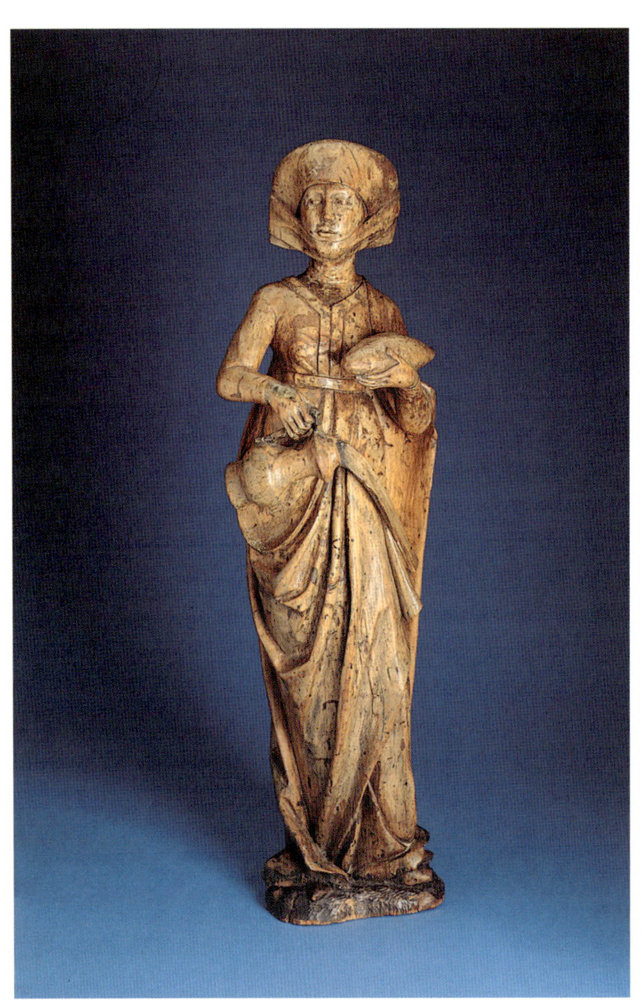

St. Elizabeth with Jug of Wine and Loaf of Bread

(ca. 1500)

Jerome Mazzaro

The anonymity of the carver

makes her uncommon attributes her own:

Not crown or habit but northern wimple

wrapping the chin establishes her rank.

Determined, slim, she stands among a poor

(not shown), turning a paused, rapt viewer charge

and us least brethren needy for her gifts.

Her arms are full, dispensing wine and bread,

negating roses that a husband saw,

 a swirling skirt wound tight about her frame.

Communion is implicit in her gifts,

On a Wood St. Elizabeth

(2000)

Jerome

Mazzaro

or that debate that Philip later set

to settle real or symbolic Presence,

reaching no agreement in the effort.

It is as if the carver's knowing knife

foresaw her central to that colloquy—

an Offertory for the Roman Mass—

and he, uncarved, her waiting enemy.

No voiceless victim she. No attribute

so overwhelms us as her caught beauty.

She is the feeling good works propagate.

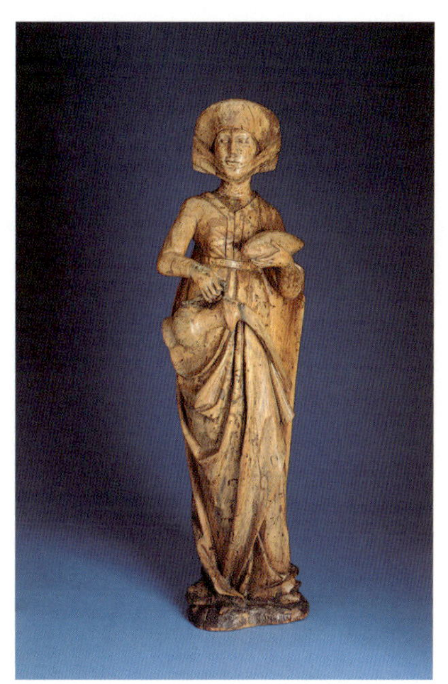

Everett Shinn

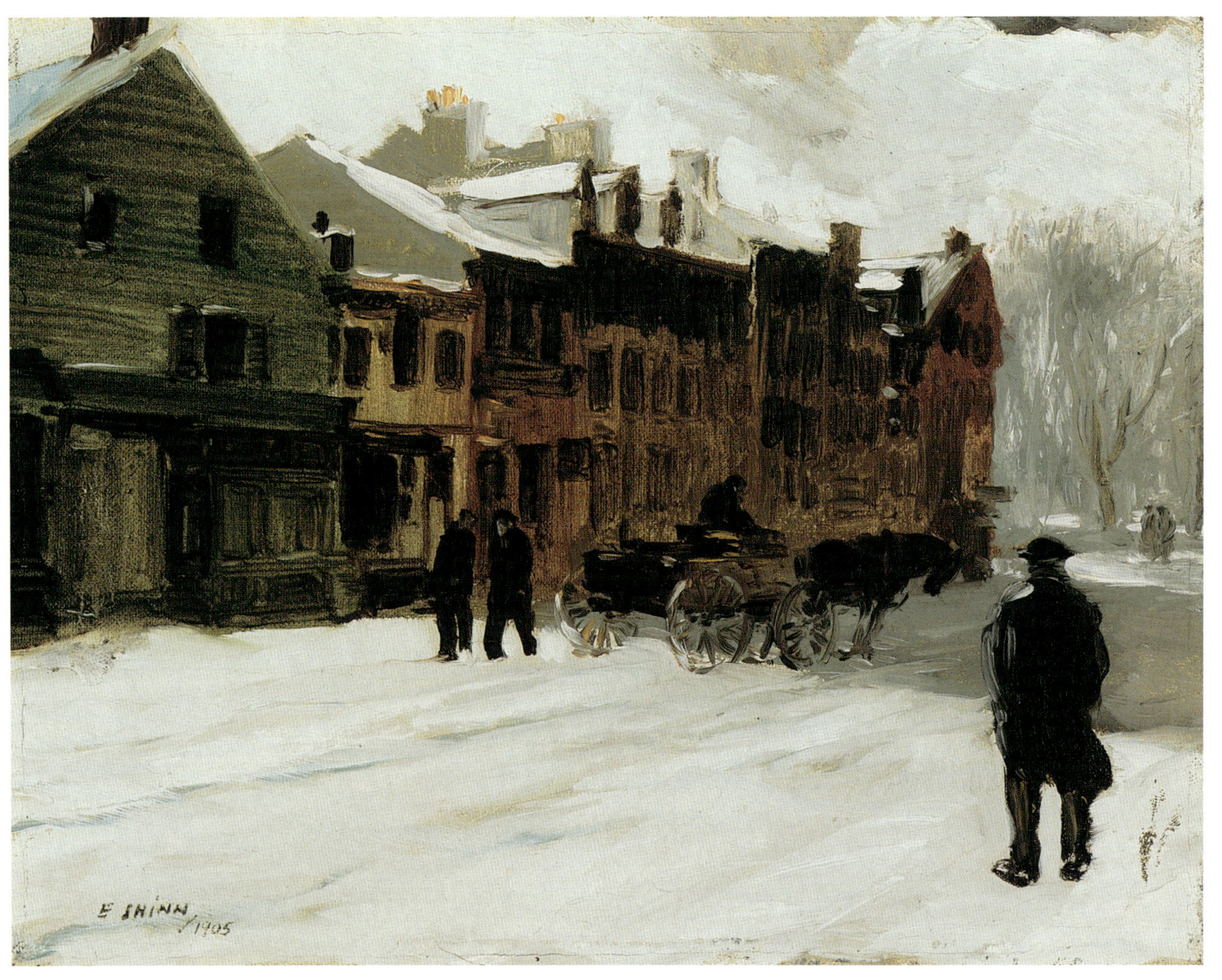

Sullivan Street

(1905)

Eleanor A. McQuilkin

It has snowed.

Coldness holds the city,

the Exchange is closed,

the Fulton Fish Market, asleep,

the ferry to New Jersey,

a far sob.

Dusk, mists rising.

Just around the corner,

Jimmy Kelly's—

cows, crows, peat, the low

stone walls of County Clare

whispering

on Sullivan Street...

Sullivan Street

(2000)

Gustave Courbet

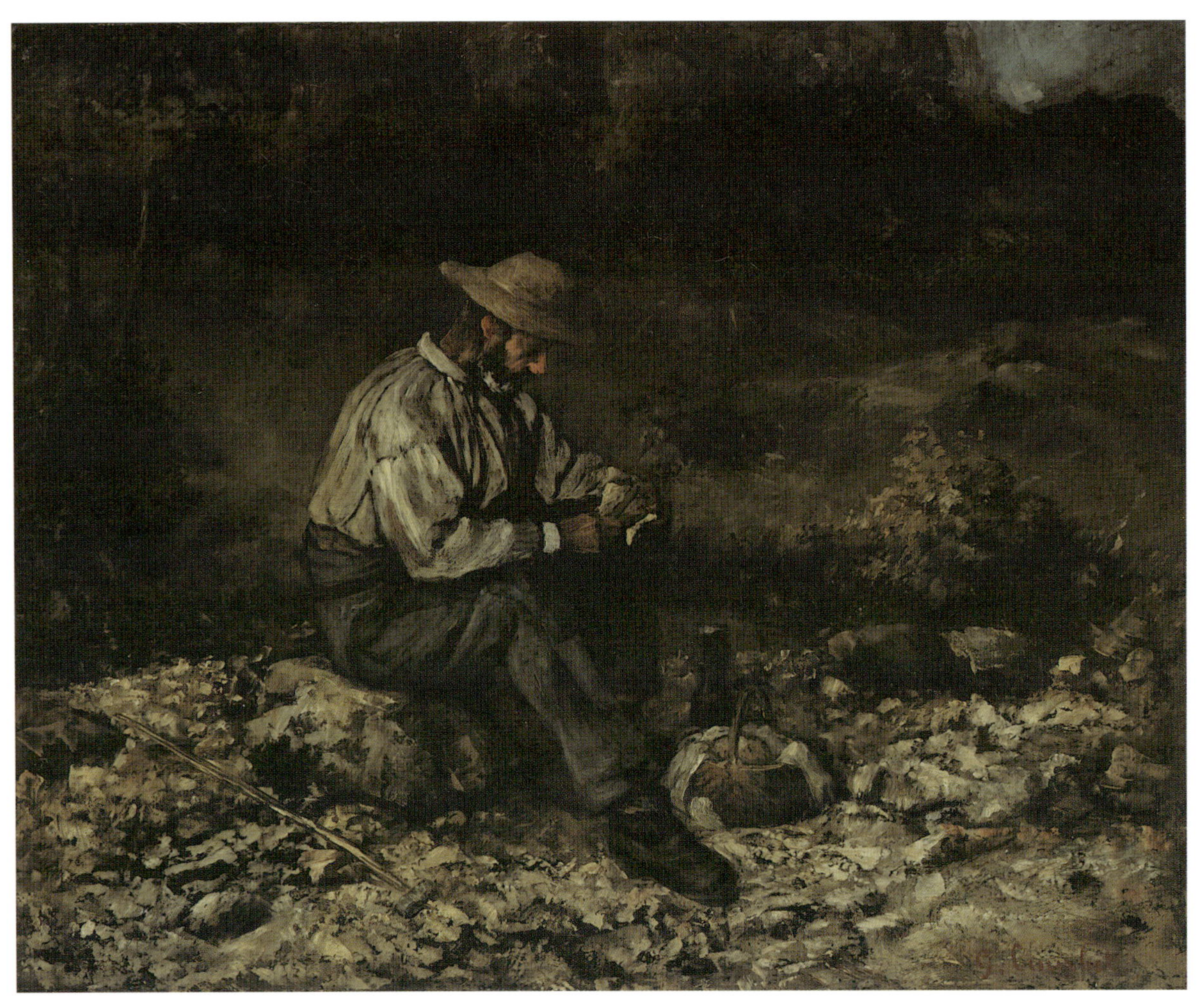

The Stonebreaker

(ca. 1872)

Rennie McQuilkin

Fixed in his frame, he lounges on
Rock, blunt boot in the foreground
Matching the dark fieldstone beyond.

His baguette, jug of ordinaire,
And hand poised to cut into cheddar
Repeat the permanence of granite.

Nothing moves. His afternoon labor
Of breaking boulders
Is out of the question. Here,

Time's no more
Than that dark coil of cloud in a far
Corner of the sky. This man in amber

Noon will always be
About to break bread and cheese
In a garden of stone, it seems—

Now the mutter of distant thunder
Tells time.

Noon at the Gallery

(2000)

Albert Bierstadt

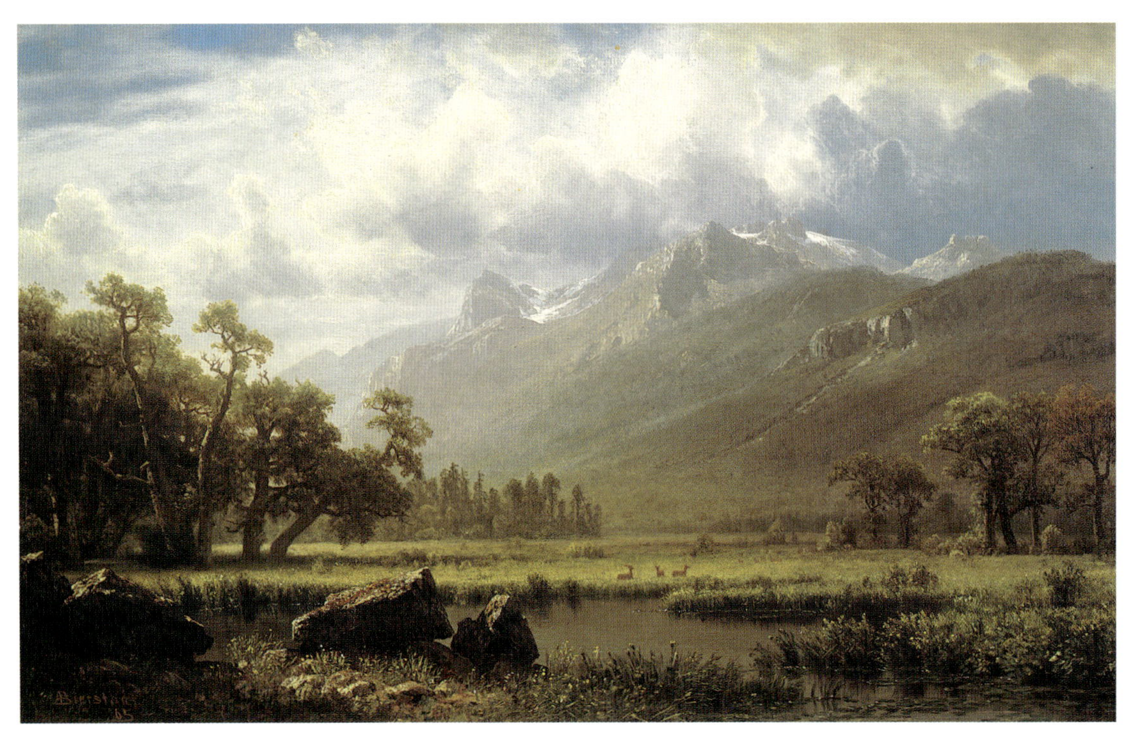

The Sierras Near Lake Tahoe, California

(1865)

Robert Morgan

"Geography has no superior to this glorious sea, this chalice of divine cloud-wine held sublimely up against the very press whence it was wrung," wrote Fitz Hugh Ludlow of Lake Tahoe. Ludlow accompanied Bierstadt on his second tour of the west in 1863, and in articles sent back to eastern magazines gave written tributes to many scenes that Bierstadt painted. It is interesting to compare Ludlow's words with Bierstadt's vistas, for I suspect that the writer wrote as the painter may have spoken of the subjects of his work.

Albert Bierstadt and the Millennium

(2000)

Bierstadt had learned his art both from his teachers at the Düsseldorf school of landscape painting and from the American masters of the Hudson River School such as Thomas Cole and Asher B. Durand. It is traditional to talk about how Bierstadt took the Edenic vision with him to the West, to "the land with no history," applying that vision to the vaster, more sublime landscape of the Rocky Mountains and the Sierras. Fitz Hugh Ludlow described it as "going to the original site of the garden of Eden." In this view the painter served as a new Adam, imaging, if not naming, the mountains and rivers, trees and animals, geysers and chasms, of the fresh new world.

But I believe this vision of an original garden is only a part of the appeal and genius of Bierstadt in his best work. His later paintings have often been described as heroic panoramas, a term that fits those works in the Capitol at Washington. But in his greatest paintings done on the second western trip, such as "The Sierras Near Lake Tahoe," there is something intimate in the foreground, and something hazy, even dreamy in the atmosphere. And the scale suggests intimacy more than spectacle.

It is a special feature of many of Bierstadt's best works that the viewer feels in the middle of the scene, not standing back from it. This is certainly true of "The Sierras Near Lake Tahoe." The viewer can almost taste the air over the pond weeds and flowers beside the water. The boulders in the foreground interrupt and complicate the scene in a lively way. The meadow appears to surround and continue behind us as we look.

But Bierstadt's art, like alchemy, is the art of far and near. What is so immediate and touchable in the foreground slides right into the farther meadow with the deer and sunlit, luminous grass. As we look at the valley floor we see a lighted plane stretching from the four bold trees on the left to the more distant clump of trees on the right. And from the base of the trees on the right we see a plane reach up over the background trees into the lit haze over the mountain flank. And from that spiritual haze on the left an even bigger plane shoots up to the snow caps and into the radiant clouds. The painter has led us in a zigzagging pattern from the humble weeds beside the still water up into the mists and celestial vapors. The painting draws us from the close and detailed to the remote and transcendental.

I do not believe the experience of this painting is essentially Edenic. I do not get a sense of looking at origins, at the past, at a lost paradise. The vision is less Adamic than prophetic. I believe Bierstadt's work is so stirring because it suggests the future, not the past. It is a painting of Pisgah vision. The viewer is looking toward the Promised Land. For Bierstadt and his contemporaries the West was destiny, the place of becoming. His paintings have the fullness of revelation. They are more Apocalyptic than nostalgic. The West is the New Jerusalem, not the lost Eden. It is a landscape lit with the beaconing future, haunted by possibility. He is looking at a world where the lion shall lie down with the lamb, in the words of Daniel. There is a sense of the culmination of a quest, not of going back to beginnings.

The painting has a sense of impending fulfillment, near the end of a long journey. Fitz Hugh Ludlow wrote of Lake Tahoe, "there, virtually at the end of our overland journey, since our feet pressed the green borders of the Golden state, we sat down to rest, feeling that one short hour, one little leap, had translated us out of the infernal world into heaven."

As we look across the buzzing meadow at the great ramp of mountain slope and lighted air, we feel something of the same translation and promise, in space haunted by haze of altar smoke catching sunlight, as if we are dreaming at the threshold of an apocalypse, at the golden frontier of the manifest Millennium.

John Koch

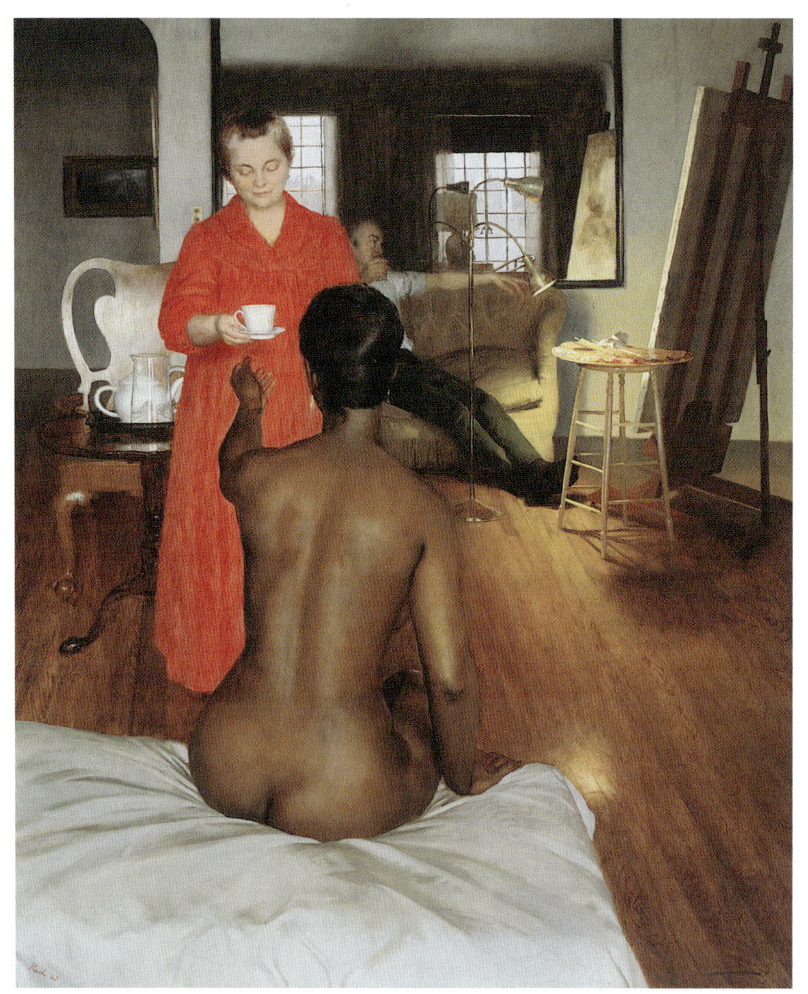

Interlude

(1963)

Joan Murray

This is between them—

the hand extending, the hand receiving,

like the great scene on the Sistine ceiling

where a single touch

ignites the clay

and Eve amazed by the naked shape

rides tucked beneath God's wing.

But it's not the creation—

which goes on in the corner

where a man turns away in his own contemplation.

And it's no annunciation,

despite the flowing red robe

of the one who's hovering

—above the one who's shivering.

Interlude

(2000)

Joan
Murray

This is only a pause

in the ongoing objectivity of the universe.

A ceremony between two women

—neither one dressed:

one nude on the edge of a rumpled bed,

and the other, plump and dimpled,

in a primly ruffled housecoat.

No, there's no intoned magnificat

—just the slow slippered steps of the artist's wife

which eternally prolong the moment

before the tea cup is released.

Her downcast gaze holds a steady course—

the cup sails forward,

balanced by equanimity.

Despite the mirror's conspiracy,

there's no way to see

what frontally greets her—

though the lambent curves of the model's back—

The Violin d'Ingres carved from mahogany,

each sinew attuned as she reaches for the tea—

suggest the symphony.

The artist sits aloof in the distance,

slumped on the hand-tufted, shirr-skirted couch,

like an onanist

who prefers his fantasy to company.
He reflects on what he's done,
rechecks his course,
rattles the ice in the glass his wife has brought.

Through the window where he's placed us,
he makes us notice as his Galatea stirs,
how the fine gold droplets on her ears
(beneath the sleek onyx sweep of her hair),
make his homey wife
in her round-shouldered robe
seem out of place and pitiful.

But if we look for some resentment
as she stands inelegant
in relation (and in service) to that loveliness,
her self-possessed air (concealing a smile),
comes forward to dismiss us,
saying, "Don't waste your pity:
she isn't what I ever wished I was—or what I've lost.

"I've stood in this room a hundred times,
offering the cup.
I've seen it sipped. Or held for warmth.
Or left there on its saucer unconsumed.
But I'm the only one he's touched.
Even now—
he's looking through the paint to find my pulse."

Thomas Cole

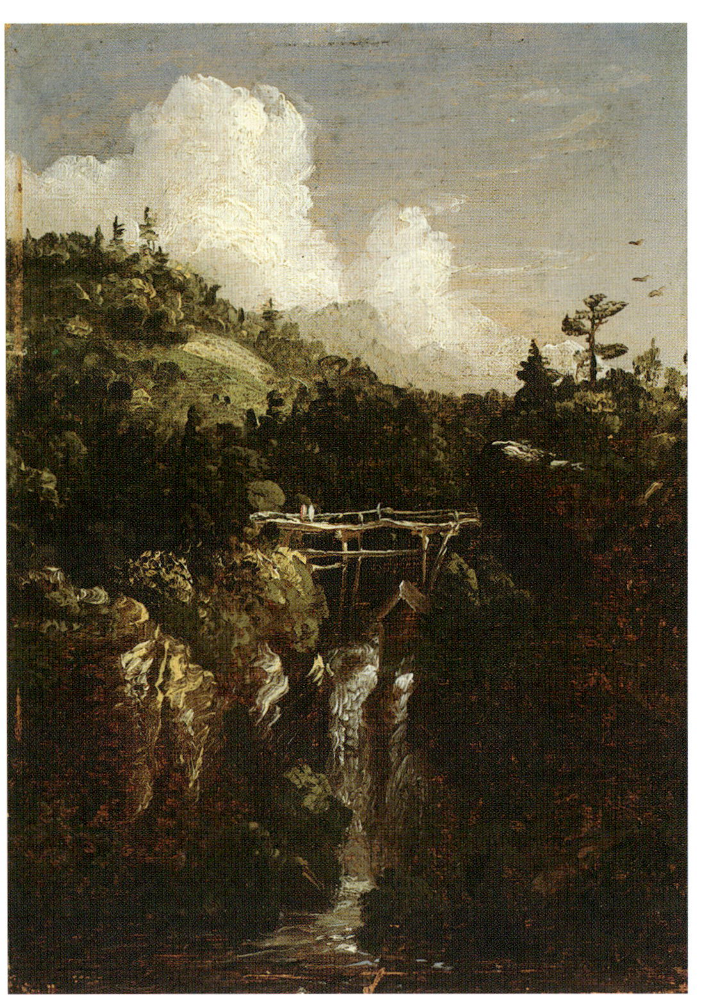

Genesee Scenery

(1846-1847)

Anthony Piccione

The tangling weave of leaf and branch releases.

We awake suddenly and at last upon a great

bristling stillness, an urge to kneel and rise

at once, as inside the chest of a cathedral.

Through the muscular rock and starkly

forested upheave a river goes on arriving.

Now the soundless clench over ears

gives way to the roaring spill of waterfall.

Entering Genesee Gorge

(2000)

Anthony

Piccione

The sky is also new, or it was always here,

strangely alive. A massive billowing cloudbank

weighs down upon all that surrounds until witness

itself enters the dark, powering, luminous presence.

Oddly heroic, then, is the squat waterwheel shack

hunched alone in its task to part the tumbling rush

and to creak on in its cogs to the grinding of bread.

Stiff, rickety, a footbridge spans the gorge and holds.

Incredibly, two robed figures, women, or monks, or angelic

visitors from another time, are walking across. Their words,

so invisible and tiny, go forth to whisper into nations.

Above them, feathery beings pause, lift upon the updraft.

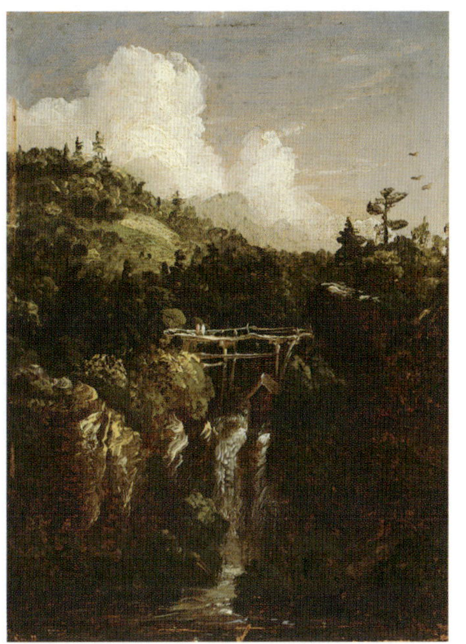

Asher Brown Durand

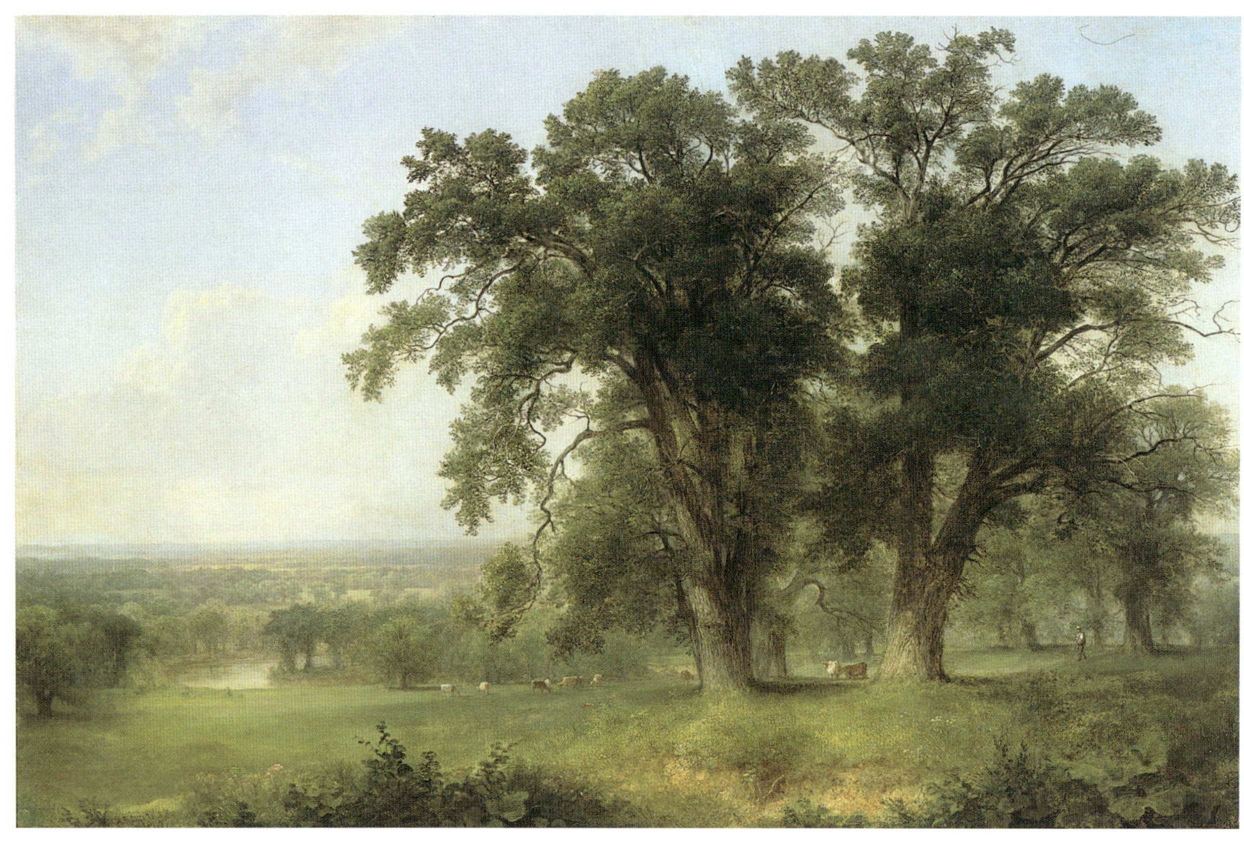

Genesee Oaks

(1860)

Jarold Ramsey

I.

Years ago, on this gallery wall, terminally

homesick for the Northwest I thought I was exiled from,

blaming Upstate New York for lacking

my birthright of mountains, deserts, junipers,

and dry horizons keeping their blue distance,

I found your painting of "Genesee Oaks,"

and looking through it like a transit began

to register the beauty and the virtue of this land.

Running West

(2000)

Jarold

Ramsey

These giant but kindly oaks, this leisurely bow-bend

in the muddy-banked river, this midday rain-shower

just lifting to heaven over Geneseo,

all in the urgent greens and shy blues

of June, composed and harmonized

in your visiting eye and hand—in these

I began to see where I really was,

a different earth under my feet, a different

sky over my head, but becoming home.

I wanted to take a map and venture forth

to discover the very place you stood to sketch

this scene in 1859, somewhere

on Squire Wadsworth's riverside acres,

as if to show myself "X—you are here!"

But of course it was a landscape of the mind

for you, addressing your big canvas in the studio,

and likewise for me, always this same glorious,

unhurried, God-given day in June.

II.

Now, a quarter-century later, steeling

myself to move on with little rituals

of goodbye like this one, I come back to your masterpiece.

It is nearly June again, and I discover

I am nearly the age you were when you painted these oaks.

Fancy that, old friend! What if now we

snatched up some of your foreground burdock,

the Seneca remedy for aches and pains,

and just galloped together into this scene you've painted,

past the man with the stick or pole on his shoulder,

past the interested cows, past the great trees themselves,

and pell mell down the irresistible

grassy slope to the river, which we skitter

across like those water-walking lizards of Borneo,

and on, you and me, running easily,

to be last seen, approaching

some far painterly vanishing point,

still running west?

Edwin Dickinson

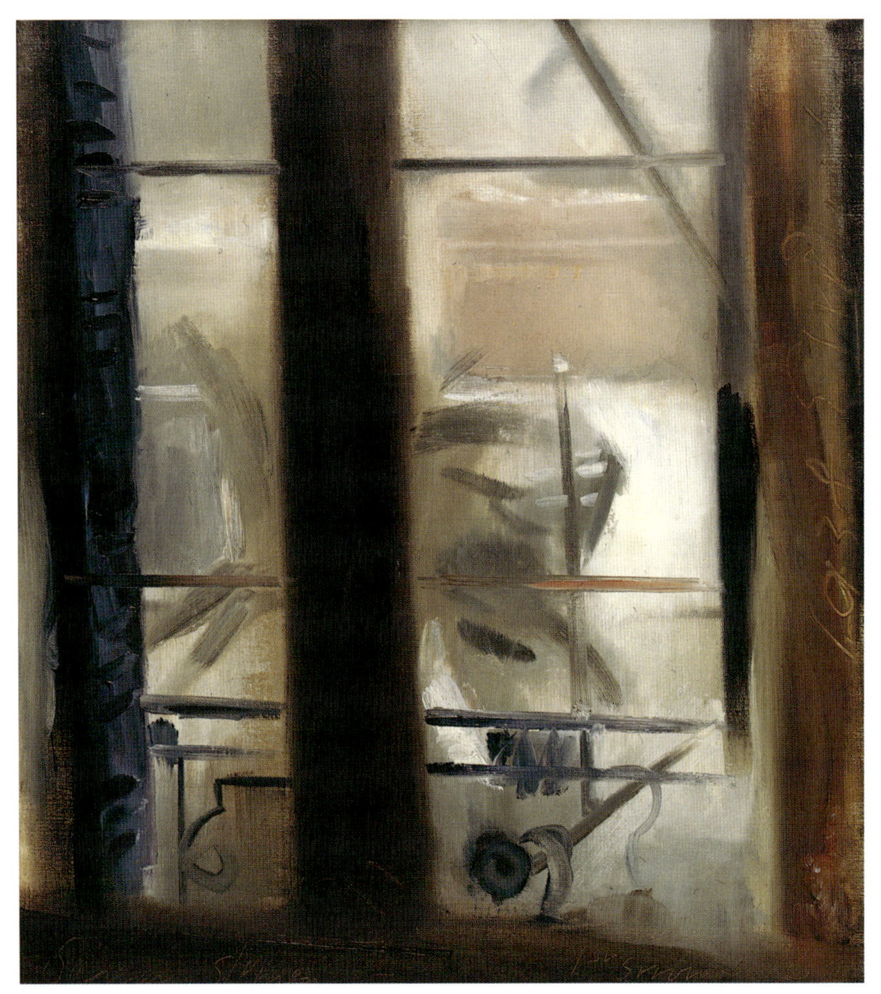

Snow on Quai, Sanary

(1938)

Stan Sanvel Rubin

Like a violin in Ravel,

they evoke

the distance you can't travel.

It is not that you don't want

to go there. You have

always wanted to go

past the vanishing point

of the pier, the dim warehouse

wavering like fog,

Blue Shutters

1st snow in 10 yrs – scratched in Edwin Dickinson's Snow on Quai, Sanary

(2000)

Stan

Sanvel Rubin

the established limit of the land

set free from itself

like an ignorance

from which you can't awaken

until you do, this time,

you do

and find yourself

lost in the pure eye,

neither in nor out

of the body, your past,

your future rushing into the space

where sky shivers and is ice.

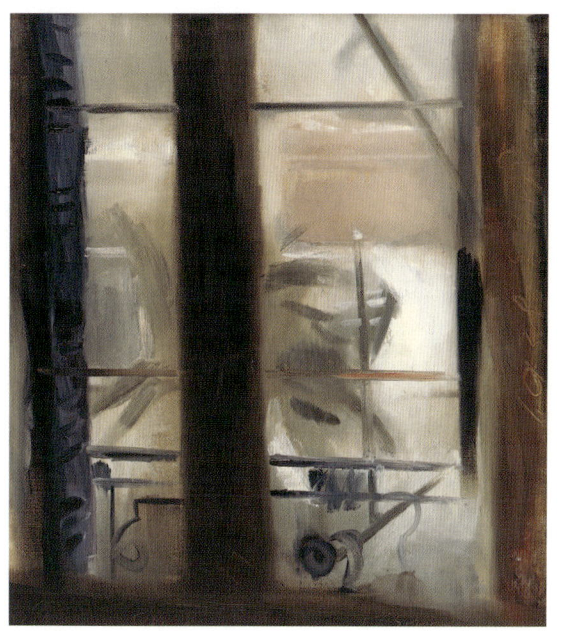

Rachel Ruysch

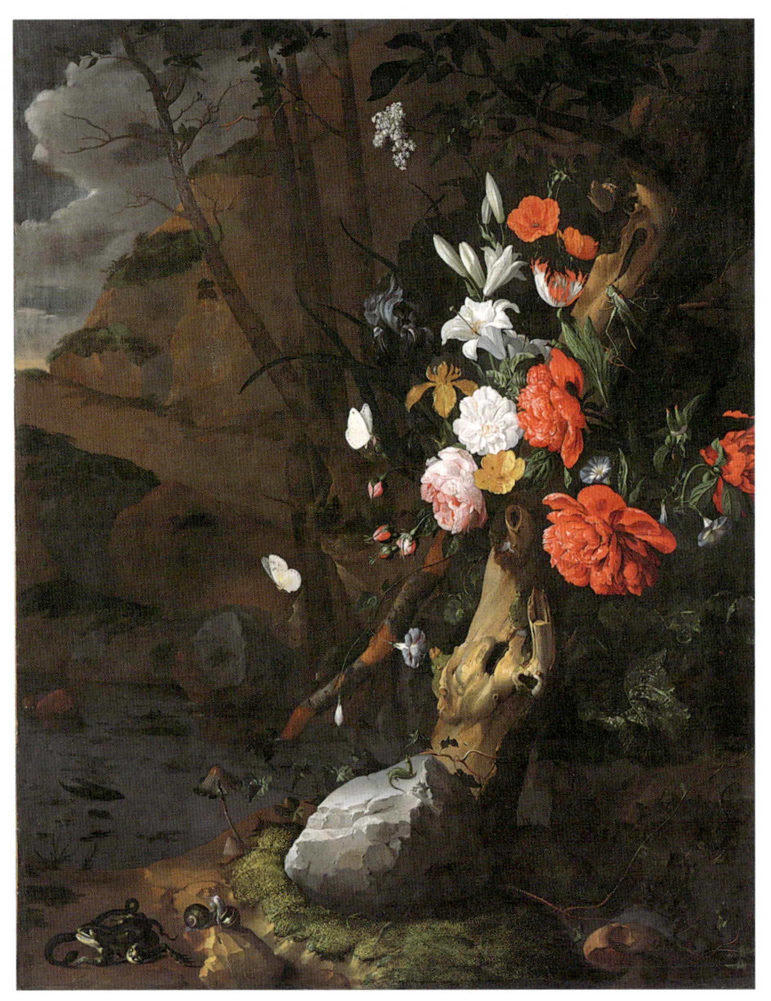

Floral Still Life

(1686)

Joanna Scott

Accidental mix of color marking

butterflies I cannot name, the yawn

of a lily and its waggling filament,

snails, toads, everything becoming

something else, a motion never

witnessed or even understood beyond

the privilege of ambition—

I did that? Dared to breed beetles,

let a snake crack a bird's egg

and lap the syrup of yolk?

Rachel Ruysch Looks Back

(2000)

Joanna

Scott

Part replica, part dream, my concoction

arranged not to impress or mollify

or earn respect but to startle—

I said that? Who gave me the right,

the method, the brushwork,

parents such as mine prepared

to buy me a master, paint, the frame,

the commission from the men

in Düsseldorf and sixty years

to dally in the marshy region of my mind—

hey ho, life, you are exquisite!

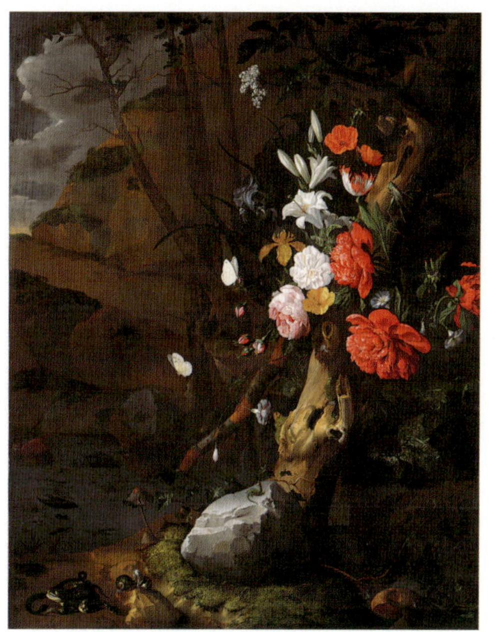

151

Winslow Homer

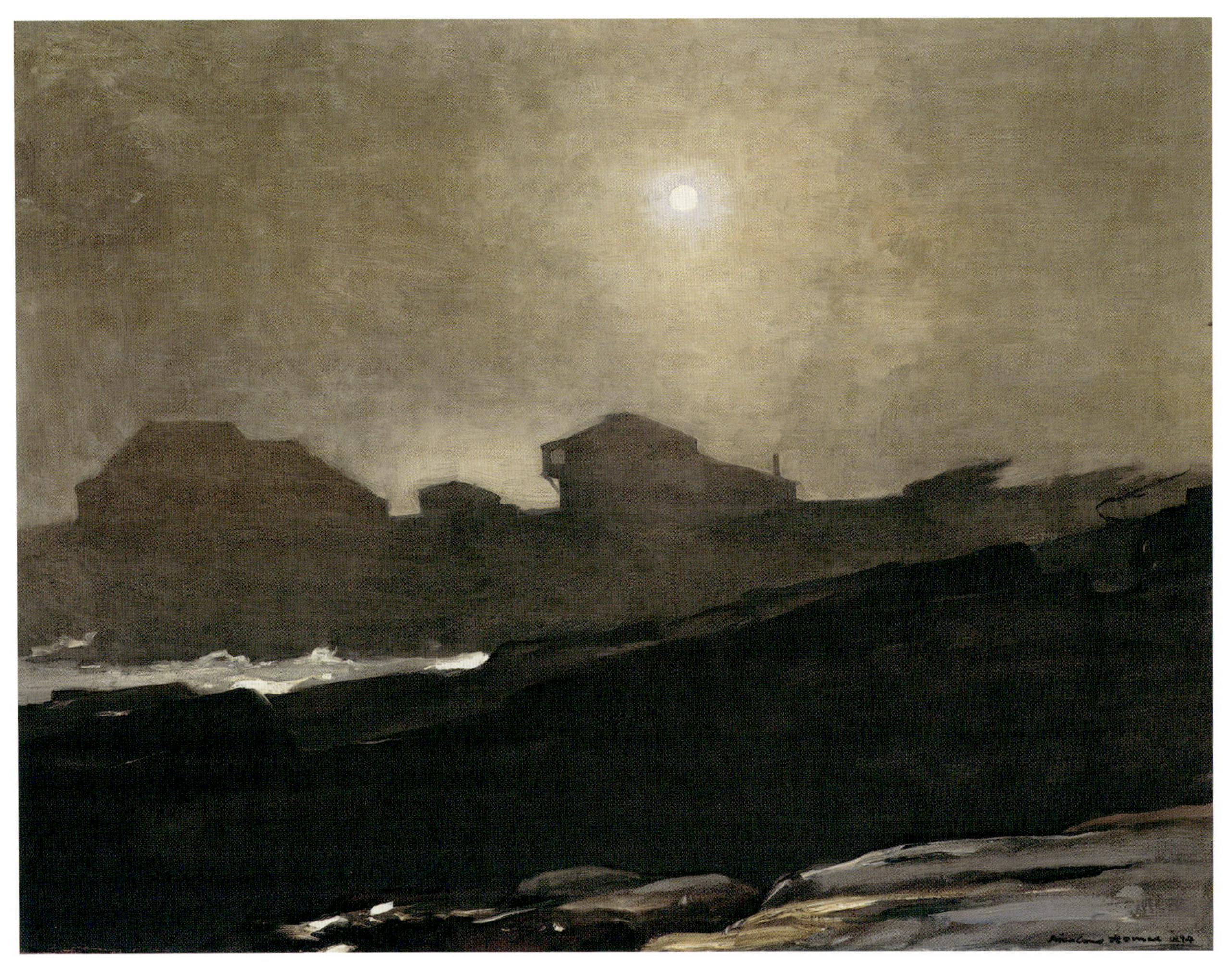

The Artist's Studio in an Afternoon Fog

(1894)

Deborah Tall

Elsewhere there are flowers,

berries, the billow

of scarves and skirts,

a fox racing a crow

for dear life.

Elsewhere women dance

or drown,

their marbled arms strained back

to smooth unruly,

floating hair.

The Artist's Studio in an Afternoon Fog
"The sun will not rise without my notice and thanks."

(2000)

But there are no more

elsewheres, only here,

where heave and undertow

unfix and claim,

where nothing

is without its use,

no color true

or constant —

nature, having lavished,

having charmed, having

horrified . . .

And so:

the sun's chill corona,

creature comforts

browned out,

prolonged seclusion

whetting your diurnal eye

to slice horizon,

fillet land from sea,

man from woman,

house from home.

And so the spindrift of

shattered light

still emitting

your careful ardor

like the heat that lingers

in lovers'

dropped clothes.

James Henry Beard

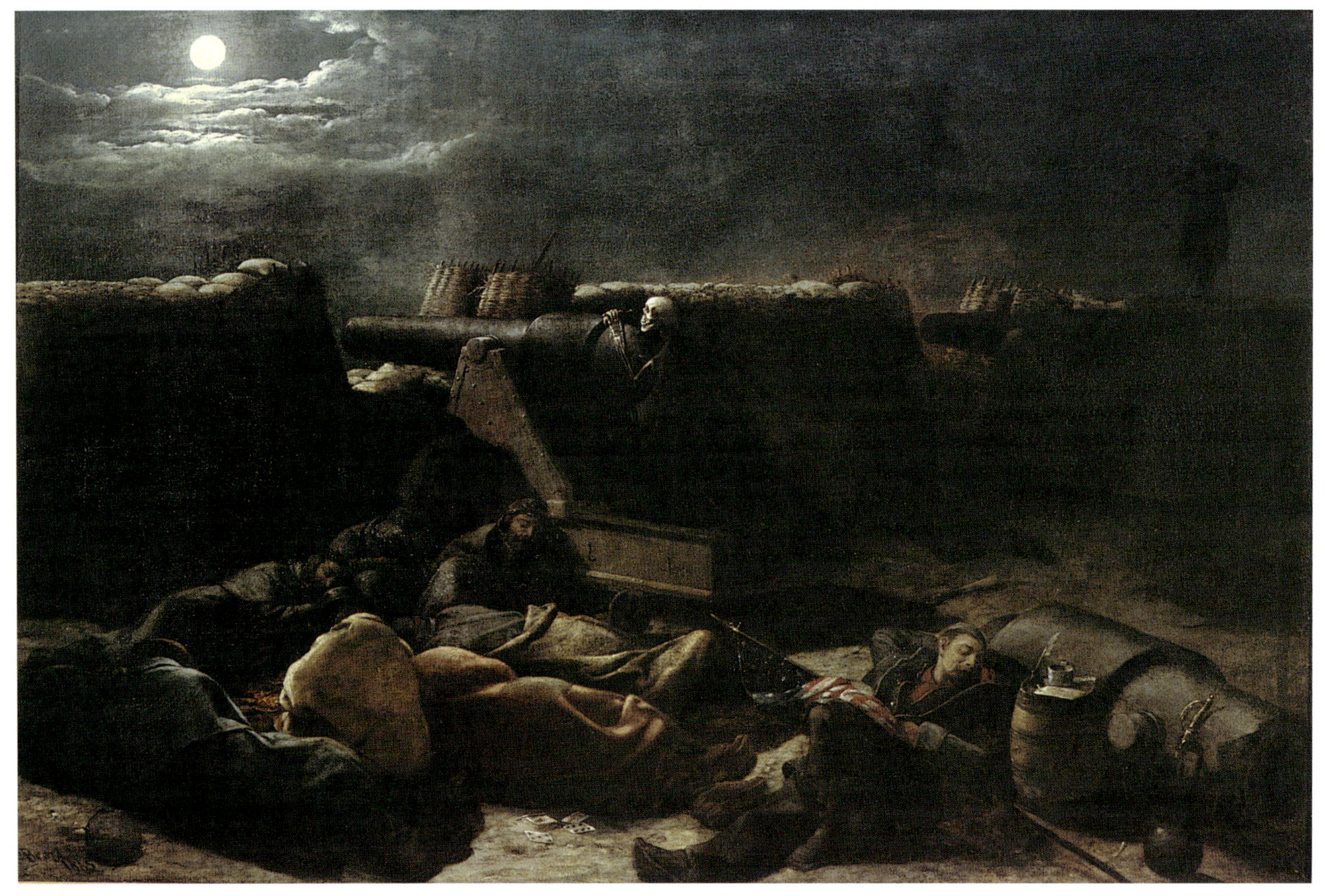

The Night Before the Battle

(1865)

Lewis Turco

The men are sleeping on the battlement.

One man reclines against a broken cannon,

Old Glory in his arms, her brilliant skirts

Lying across his thigh. He is content,

One may assume. It's hard to see the others

Scattered among the shadows strewn like stone

Across the night, although the moonlight flirts

With the outlines of this rallying of Brothers-

James Henry Beard: The Night Before the Battle, 1865

(2000)

In-Arms. One must look close to count those who

Are most obscure. Some seem to disappear

Nearly to nothing. "Nearly" is not the word,

For one can just perceive the stone wall through

The body of this man who sits, his poll

Resting upon his knees — some gathered here

Are phantom sleepers who will once more gird

Their loins and hearts in answer to the call

That dawn will bring ringing along the pall

Of mist beneath the moon flooding the fields

Below with the cold immensity of dream.

Two are awake: one of them, on the wall,

Stands lookout dressed like Banquo's ghost

And stares into the night. What power he wields

With his ancient eye is moot, for its piercing beam

Is turned away from us. He stands his post

Listening, but does the other sentinel

See and hear more clearly? — he sights along

The barrel of a cannon aiming out

Into the umber brooding within the well

Of stillness beneath the moon. His empty sockets

Stare at nothingness. He hears the song

Of death echoing in his skull, the shout

Of the charging shades and of the bursting rockets —

Soon his comrades must rise up in a host

And, like his own, their moonlit dreams be lost.

Walter Murch

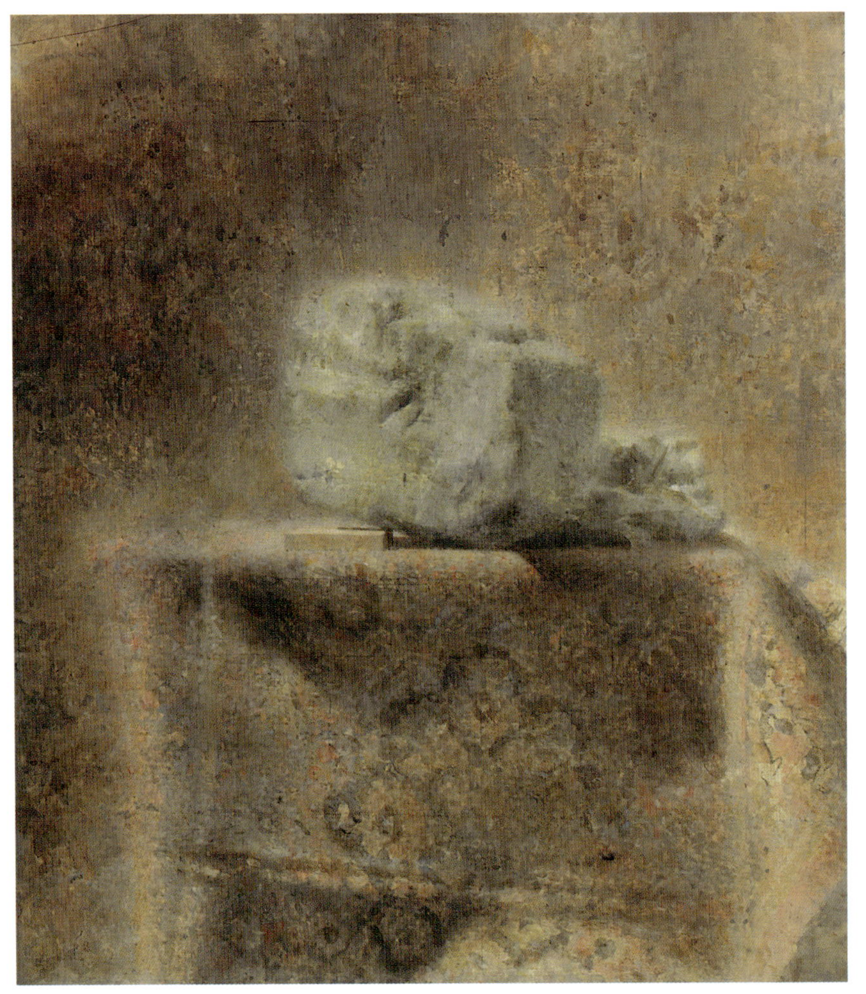

Resting Rock

(1961)

Kathleen Wakefield

1. *A Man Lays a Rug on a Table*

   and a Rock on the Rug to See What It Might Be

For a while he is confused by the light. From nowhere
and everywhere. And the single line of shadow the rock
casts so that it seems to be made of nothing. How the rock
fills the room with the bleached scrapings of beetle legs,
the slow shine of grit and dust, ashes of an old fire.
He knows it's not gravity that holds the rock to the rough
wool it rests on: those dark shallows where huge fish
lumber, riverbeds flashed with turquoise and gold
a boy dreamed. And still he's surprised by the rock's cool
radiance, his head grown heavy as if to bow before what he
did not make.

Resting Rock

(2000)

Kathleen

Wakefield

2. *The Rock Remembers When It Was Not There*

   and When It Was Taken Away

The rock in the field did not dispute

the wind nor the grass streamers drawn over its face.

The rock never once laid claim to the dry shadows of August,

held nothing against the telegraphic

clicking of red ants.

Some days the rock blazed up singing about the chain

of sorrows beginning long before the crippled farmhand

came to sit at its side and the second crop failed.

Like a great engine lifted from the earth

it hummed the original velocity of the stars,

songs of measurement and watercourses

and the slow slaking away.

The rock was the touch of the man's hand

and the sun, and the quick, dry body

of the red and black striped king snake

draped over its granite torso.

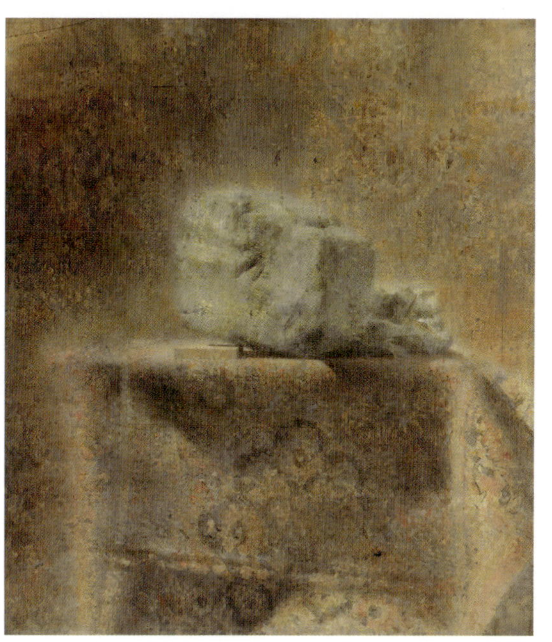

Nancy S. Graves

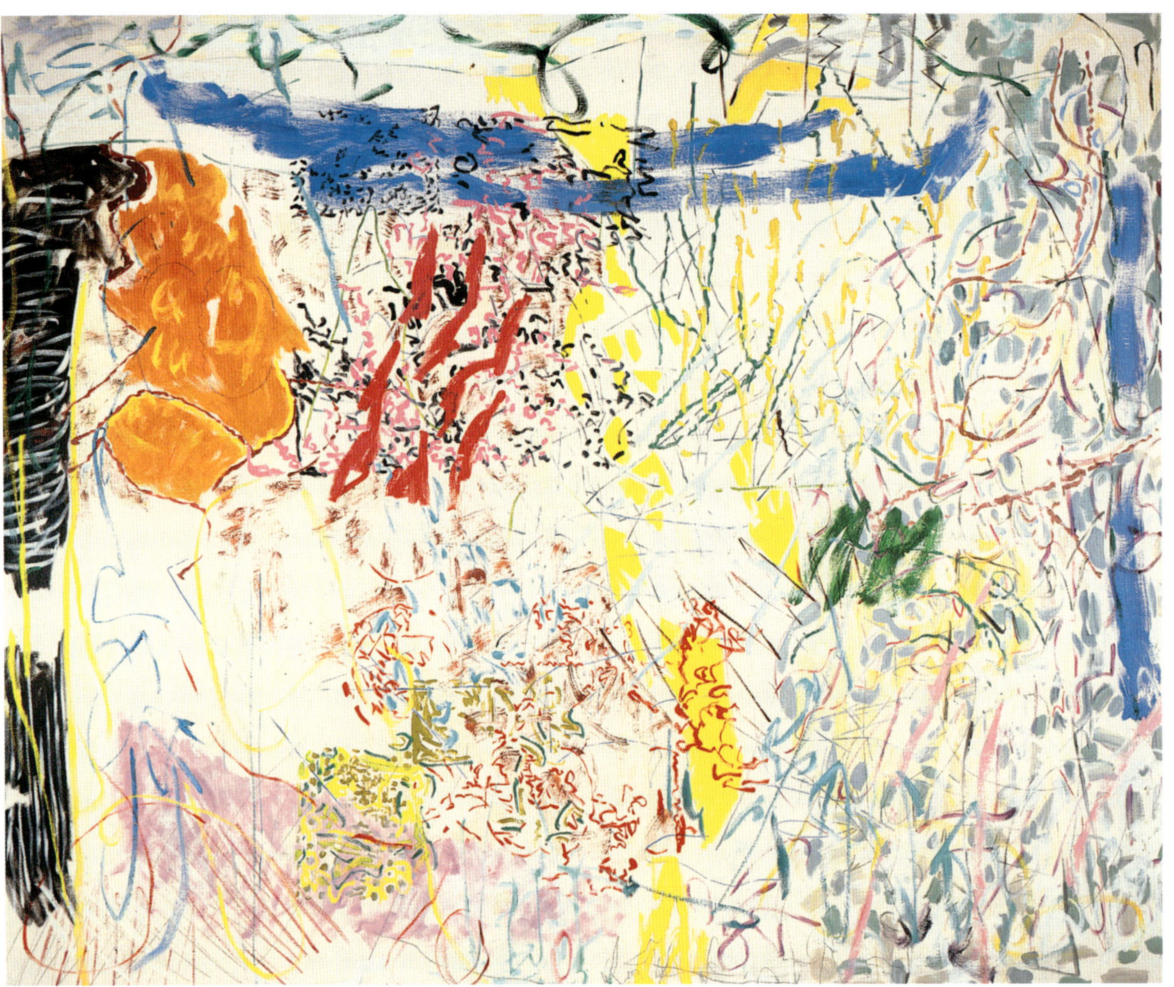

Nancy Graves, *Fragment*, 1977. © Nancy Graves Foundation/Licensed by VAGA, New York, NY.

Fragment

(1977)

Thom Ward

The wind puts its ladder against the house

and blows milky songs across your hip

that trombones retrieve and echo off industrious

boats. The gods of dairy products once inhabited

this spot, left the charts they used to excavate

the Ruins of Nonchalant, the moxie to crack open

littlenecks and hazelnuts. *Translatus, translatus,*

let's disappear beneath the bashful scarecrows

of hanging folders. When the southpaw thumps

American Fragment

(2000)

the slugger on the head, how soon the romantic

becomes the self-righteous. Why not create promotions

for bric-a-brac nobody wants. Because my tonsils

look like tractor tires my dentist has purchased

a dismemberment plan, and the sheriff who reads

to incarcerated mice does so in fleeced pajamas.

Ersatz or whiteout, I'll take whatever's possible,

though, honestly, I'd rather swap amino acids

and the fictions roped to the bill of a turbulent duck

who's memorized the postal zips of faraway folks.

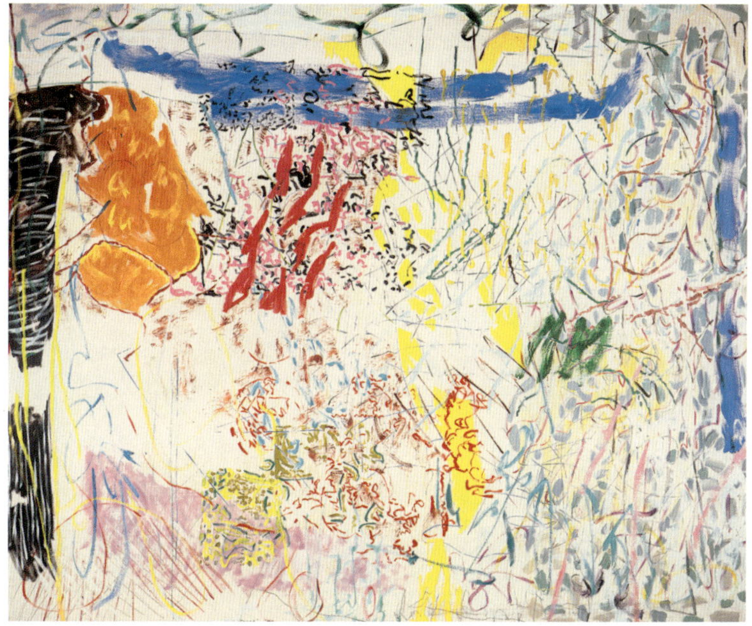

Nancy Graves, *Fragment*, 1977. © Nancy Graves Foundation/Licensed by VAGA, New York, NY.

John Henry Twachtman

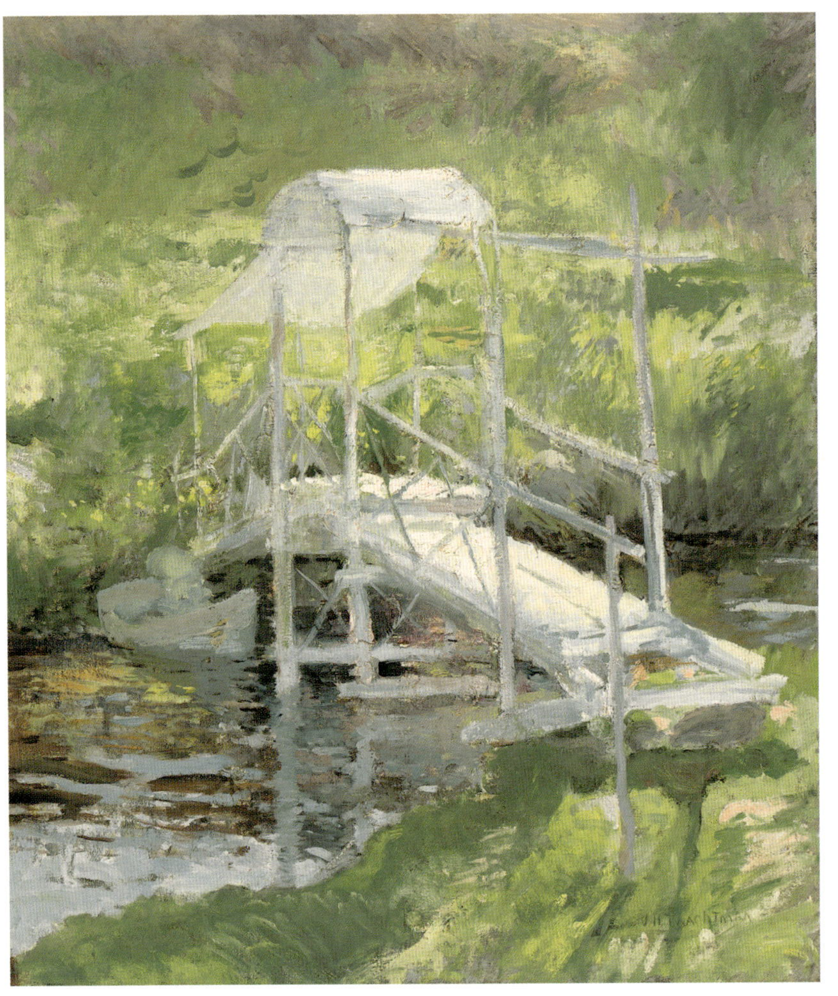

The White Bridge

(ca. 1900)

David Weiss

Dear Grant Holcomb,

It pains me to tell you this,

but I never did get to the museum

to find a piece of art to write about.

(No doubt, for effect, I should save

this damning admission the way Robert

Frost does in his eponymous poem

about Vermont when he lets on only

at the very end that he himself doesn't

live there at all but in New Hampshire.)

However, the other day, a bridge —

A Sin of Commission

(2000)

David
Weiss

John Henry Twachtman's robustly delicate,

turn of the century "The White Bridge"

which I came across in the U. of R.

Memorial Art Gallery's summary catalogue,

1977 – saved me from the sin of omission

for a different sin: angled across

the foreground, with rowboat tied to it,

a wooden footbridge leads into

a meadow, pathless, seedy and wanton

as only a painter can make you feel

about it: you just want to walk

into that lush, blowzy day, and only

this bridge can get you there – the punt's

by the far bank, the current calmly

swift: you'll have to cross this half-

covered, or maybe just half-

built bridge (it's hard to tell

from the half-tone reproduction) but

not before you notice in the boat

turned athwart the stream a woman

in a white dress you hadn't observed

before (a consequence of the 5 X 3

reduction onto cream-colored paper,

but also the painting's impressionism),

her languid arm moored fast to,

indistinguishable from, the bridge

itself, her body fused with the boat

like a kayaker or mermaid, the smoky

brush strokes of her dress of a piece

with the greenery behind, the dress

the same hue as the bridge glittering

on the water's nervy surface –

no wonder I'd missed her. So easily

erect she sits, and patient, as

though she knows that enough may not

be possible but that more than enough

often is, occurring without

drama or fanfare, sometimes just by

walking out onto a white bridge

above a softly roiling stream and feeling,

because it's pure apprehension,

that this summer day is full to brimming –

there, inexhaustibly, for the taking,

just by taking it in.

      I'm glad this poor

Platonic copy of Twachtman's painting is all

I have before me: neither color nor texture

can I make out nor the mien of expectant

pleasure on the woman's face as she

gazes upstream beyond the painter's ken.

I can't tell if this moment is enough for her

or too much or if she's simply waiting

for someone to reappear. Which is

a relief. The little I can see, all by itself,

is already almost too much to bear.

Notes on Contributors

KATH M. ANDERSON
has taught poetry at Empire State College, Rochester Institute of Technology, the State University of New York College at Brockport, and Writers & Books in Rochester. She has published two chapbooks: *An Abbreviated History of Water* and *Hauling Water*.

JOHN ASHBERY
was born in Rochester, New York, and grew up in nearby Sodus. As a child he attended classes in the Creative Workshop of the Memorial Art Gallery. He has written more than twenty books of poetry, including *Self-Portrait in a Convex Mirror* (1975), which received the Pulitzer Prize for poetry, the National Book Award, the National Book Critics Circle Award and the Poetry Society of America's Robert Frost Medal. His books on art include *Reported Sightings* (1991) and *Girls on the Run: A Poem*, a meditation on the paintings of "Outsider" artist Henry Darger. His most recent book is *Other Traditions* (2000). A Guggenheim and MacArthur Fellow, he has served as Chancellor of the Academy of American Poets.

ANDREA BARRETT
a resident of Rochester, has written five novels, including *The Voyage of the Narwhal* (1998). Her book of short stories, *Ship Fever and Other Stories*, won the National Book Award for Fiction in 1996. She teaches in the MFA Program for Writers at Warren Wilson College.

TODD BEERS
is currently Poet in Residence at Monroe County Children's Center, a facility for incarcerated teens, as well as a visiting artist in outreach programs for area schools and universities. He is editor of over a dozen anthologies of children's poetry, including *Waiting Room: Writings By Children and Adult Patients in a Hospital Setting*. His own work has been published in numerous journals, anthologies and chapbooks.

MARVIN BELL
attended Alfred University and Syracuse University and is currently Flannery O'Connor Professor of Letters at the Writers' Workshop at the University of Iowa. Author of many books of poetry and essays (including the recently published *Nightworks: Poems 1962-2000*), Bell has been awarded the Lamont Prize by the Academy of American Poets and an Award in Literature from the American Academy of Arts and Letters. He has held two Senior Fulbright appointments and has been honored by, among others, the Guggenheim Foundation and the National Endowment for the Arts.

BRUCE BENNETT
is Professor of English and Director of the Creative Writing Program at Wells College in Aurora, New York. He is the author of fifteen chapbooks and four volumes of poetry, most recently *Navigating the Distances: Poems New and Selected* (Orchises, 1999). He co-founded and served as editor of *Ploughshares* and *Field: Contemporary Poetry and Poetics* and is Associate Editor at State Street Press.

CHARLES BERNSTEIN
is David Gray Professor of Poetry and Letters and Director of the Poetics Program at the State University of New York at Buffalo. He has written over twenty books of poetry and several collections of essays, including *My Way: Speeches and Poems* (1999) and *Republics of Reality: 1975-1995* (2000). Editor of *Close Listening: Poetry and the Performed Word*, he has also written librettos with composers Ben Yarmolinsky, Dean Drummond and Brian Ferneyhough.

KATE BRAVERMAN
resides in Alfred, New York, and is the author of three novels, four books of poetry and two collections of short stories. "Tall Tales from the Mekong Delta" was in *Best American Short Stories of 1991*, and won the O. Henry Award in 1992. "Pagan Night" was in *Best American Short Stories of 1995*.

JOSEPH BRUCHAC
a resident of Greenfield, New York, is a poet, storyteller and writer who often draws upon his Native American (Abenaki) heritage. In addition to his many award-winning children's books, he has written two novels (*Dawn Land* and *Long River*), a collection of essays (*Roots of Survival: Native American Storytelling and the Sacred*), and a memoir (*Bowman's Store: A Journey to Myself*). He has won the PEN Syndicated Fiction Award and the American Book Award.

HAYDEN CARRUTH
lives in upstate New York where he taught in the Graduate Creative Writing Program at Syracuse University. In addition to his many books of poetry, he has written a novel, four books of criticism and two anthologies. *Collective Shorter Poems, 1946-1991* won the National Book Critics Circle Award, and *Scrambled Eggs and Whiskey* received the National Book Award for Poetry in 1996. Carruth has received fellowships from the Bollingen Foundation and the National Endowment for the Arts, as well as a Lannan Literary Fellowship. He was awarded the Vermont Governor's Medal and, among others, the Shelley Memorial Award, the Harriet Monroe Award, the Lenore Marshall Award, the Paterson Poetry Prize and the Carl Sandburg Award.

ZENA COLLIER
was born in London and now resides in Rochester, New York. Her short stories and nonfiction have appeared in many magazines and journals, and she has written two novels, *Ghost Note* and *A Cooler Climate*. The latter was made into a Showtime movie which aired in 1999.

ROBERT CREELEY

Samuel P. Capen Professor of Poetry and Humanities at the State University of New York at Buffalo, has written over sixty books of poetry, a novel, essays, interviews and numerous short stories. He has been the subject of numerous critical studies, including *Robert Creeley's Life and Work: A Sense of Increment.* The University of California Press has published *The Collected Poems of Robert Creeley, 1945-1975* (1982), *The Collected Essays of Robert Creeley* (1989) and *Selected Poems* (1991). His recent books of poems, *Echoes, Life & Death* (1998) and *So There: Poems 1976-83*, were published by New Directions. Creeley's awards include the Frost Medal, the Shelley Memorial Award and, in 1999, the Bollingen Prize. He was New York State Poet from 1989 to 1991 and, in 1996, elected a Chancellor of the Academy of American Poets. He is a member of the American Academy of Arts and Letters.

CORNELIUS EADY

was born in Rochester, New York. He is the author of four books of poetry, including *Gathering of My Name* (1991), a Pulitzer Prize nominee, and *Victims of the Latest Dance Craze,* which won the Lamont Poetry Prize in 1985. His most recent book is *Brutal Imagination* (2000). Eady has received the Prairie Schooner Strousse Award and fellowships from the Guggenheim Foundation, the National Endowment for the Arts, the Rockefeller Foundation and the Lila Wallace-Readers Digest Foundation. He is Associate Professor of English and Director of the Poetry Center at the State University of New York at Stony Brook.

THOMAS GAVIN

Professor Emeritus of English at the University of Rochester, is the author of three novels, *Kingkill, The Last Film of Emile Vico* and *Breathing Water.* He is a Bread Loaf Writers' Conference Fellow, National Endowment for the Arts Creative Writing Fellow, Mellon Faculty Fellow and winner of the Lillian Fairchild Award for distinguished achievement in the arts.

ANTHONY HECHT

former John H. Deane Professor of Poetry and Rhetoric at the University of Rochester, is the author of many books of poetry, including *The Hard Hours,* winner of the Pulitzer Prize in 1967. His critical studies include *The Hidden Law: The Poetry of W. H. Auden, On the Laws of Poetic Art: The Andrew Mellon Lectures, 1992* (1995) and *Obbligati: Essays in Criticism* (1996). Among his many awards and honors are the Bollingen Prize, the Ruth Lilly Prize, the Librex-Guggenheim Eugenio Montale Award, the Harriet Monroe Poetry Award and fellowships from the American Academy of Poets, the American Academy in Rome, and the Ford, Guggenheim and Rockefeller Foundations. He has served as Consultant in Poetry to the Library of Congress and is currently Chancellor Emeritus of the Academy of American Poets.

WILLIAM HEYEN

is Professor Emeritus of English at the State University of New York College at Brockport, where he served as Poet in Residence for many years. Heyen has written many books of poetry, essays and fiction. Recent publications include *Pig Notes & Dumb Music: Prose on Poetry* and *Crazy Horse in Stillness*, which won the Small Press Book Award for Poetry in 1997. A former Senior Fulbright lecturer on American literature in Germany, he has also received fellowships from the National Endowment for the Arts, the Guggenheim Foundation and the American Academy and Institute of Arts and Letters.

SUSAN HOLAHAN

is a former lawyer, journalist and teacher of writing at Yale and the University of Rochester. Her poetry has appeared in *Crazyhorse, Agni, The Women's Review of Books;* her fiction in *American Short Fiction, Icarus*—and many others. Her book, *Sister Betty Reads the Whole You*, won the 1998 Peregrine Smith Poetry Prize.

BEN HOWARD

is author of five books, including the verse novella *Midcentury* (1997) and *The Pressed Melodeon: Essays on Modern Irish Writing.* His forthcoming book, *Dark Pool*, is expected in 2002. He has received numerous awards, including the Milton Dorfman Prize. A recipient of a fellowship from the National Endowment for the Arts, he is Professor of English at Alfred University, where he teaches literature, writing and classical guitar.

SUSAN HOWE

is Professor of English at the State University of New York at Buffalo. Her books of poetry include *Singularities* (1990), *The Europe of Trusts: Selected Poems* (1990), *Frame Structures: Early Poems 1974-1979* (1996) and most recently *Pierce-Arrow* (1999). She is also the author of two books of literary criticism, *My Emily Dickinson* (1985) and *The Birth-Mark: Unsettling the Wilderness in American Literary History* (1993). She lives in Guilford, Connecticut.

STEVEN HUFF

is Publisher/Managing Editor of BOA Editions, Ltd. in Rochester, New York. His fiction has been published in *American Short Fiction, The Pushcart Prizes: Best of the Small Presses XX*, and *Chelsea.* His poetry has appeared in *Kentucky Poetry Review, Bitterroot* and *Painted Bride Quarterly.*

M.J. IUPPA

lives on a small farm near Lake Ontario. Recent poems have appeared in *Poetry, Tar River Poetry, The Comstock Review* and elsewhere; her creative non-fiction is included in *In Brief: Short Takes on the Personal*, edited by Judith Kitchen and Mary Paumier Jones (W.W. Norton, 1999), and *Chelsea*. Her chapbooks are *Sometimes Simply* (Foreseeable Future Press, 1996) and *Temptations* (Foothills Publishing, 2001). She is Writer in Residence at St. John Fisher College, and curates The Genesee Reading Series at Writers & Books, Rochester, New York.

BRUCE A. JACOBS

was born and raised in Rochester. His first book of poetry, *Speaking Through My Skin*, won the Naomi Long Madgett Poetry Prize in 1996. His writing has appeared in *American Writing, African-American Review* and *Beloit Poetry Journal*. His most recent book, *Race Manners: Navigating the Minefield Between Black and White Americans* (1999), was featured on National Public Radio.

BARBARA JORDAN

is Associate Professor of English at the University of Rochester. She won the Barnard New Women Poets Prize in 1989 for her first volume of poetry, *Channel. Trace Elements* was published in 1998. Jordan has won the Grolier Poetry Prize and received fellowships from the National Endowment for the Arts, the Massachusetts Artists Foundation and the Bread Loaf Writers' Conference.

JUDITH KITCHEN

is Writer in Residence at the State University of New York College at Brockport. She is the author of *Perennials*, a collection of poems; *Only the Dance: Essays on Time and Memory*; and a second collection of personal essays, *Distance and Direction* (Coffee House Press, 2001). She co-edited *In Short: A Collection of Brief Creative Nonfiction* and *In Brief: Short Takes on the Personal* (W.W. Norton). Her critical study of William Stafford (*Writing the World: Understanding William Stafford*) was reprinted by Oregon State University Press in l999. A recipient of the Pushcart Prize and a National Endowment for the Arts Fellowship, she is a regular reviewer of poetry for *The Georgia Review*.

JIM LAVILLA-HAVELIN

was born in New York City and raised in Rochester, New York. He worked in the Education Department of the Memorial Art Gallery from 1979 to 1986, eventually serving as the Gallery's Curator of Education. Jim is the author of three books of poetry. He was the founding Director of the San Antonio Children's Museum, and is currently the Director of the Young Artist Programs at the Southwest School of Art & Craft.

JAMES LONGENBACH

is Joseph H. Gilmore Professor of English at the University of Rochester and author of the critical studies *Stone Cottage: Pound, Yeats and Modernism; Wallace Stevens: The Plain Sense of Things;* and, most recently, *Modern Poetry After Modernism*. His poems have appeared in *The Nation, The New Republic, Paris Review* and *The Best American Poetry 1995*. His first book of poetry, *Threshold*, was published in 1998.

JEROME MAZZARO

a literary critic and poet, retired from the State University of New York at Buffalo in 1996. His critical studies include works on Dante, as well as on classical, Renaissance and modern literature. His poems have been published in *The Hudson Review, The Literary Review, The Ohio Review, Salmagundi* and *Modern Poetry Studies*. His books of poetry include *Changing the Windows* (1966) as well as *The Caves of Love* and *Rubbings*, both published in 1985.

ELEANOR A. MCQUILKIN

a long-time resident of Rochester, New York, is author of three books of poetry: *Mornings* (1986), *Every Sky* (1998) and *Grip* (2000), a collaboration with Rochester artist Robert Marx. McQuilkin has served as President of the Rochester Poetry Society and has been an active member of The Book Club, Friends of the University of Rochester Libraries, and Writers & Books.

RENNIE MCQUILKIN

a Rochester native, has published his poetry in *The Atlantic Monthly, The Southern Review, Poetry* and *The Yale Review*. He is the author of two books of poetry, *North Northeast* and *We All Fall Down*, winner of the 1986 Swallow's Tale Poetry Award. A former teacher of English at the Phillips Academy and Miss Porter's School, he is the founding director of the Sunken Garden Poetry Festival in Connecticut.

ROBERT MORGAN

Professor of English at Cornell University, has written many books of poetry, a volume of short stories and several novels, including *Gap Creek: The Story of a Marriage*, which was an Oprah Book Club Selection and winner of the Southern Book Critics Circle Award for Fiction in 2000. *The Truest Pleasure* (published in 1995 and reprinted in 1999) was a finalist for the Southern Book Critics Circle Award for Fiction and was listed by *Publisher's Weekly* as one of the outstanding books of 1995. He has received the Southern Poetry Review Prize, the Eunice Tiefjens Award, the Jacaranda Review Fiction Prize and the North Carolina Award in Literature.

JOAN MURRAY

a former resident of Rochester and Buffalo, is Poet in Residence for the New York State Writers Institute at the State University of New York at Albany. Her newest books are *Looking for the Parade* (W.W. Norton, 1999), which won the National Poetry Series competition, and *Queen of the Mist: the Forgotten Heroine of Niagara* (Beacon, 1999), which she has adapted for Broadway's Jujamcyn Theaters. She is also winner of the Poetry Society of America's Gordon Barber Award, a Pushcart Prize, and fellowships from the National Endowment for the Arts and the New York Foundation for the Arts.

ANTHONY PICCIONE

is Emeritus Professor of English and Creative Writing at the State University of New York College at Brockport. He has published four chapbooks and three volumes of poetry. *Anchor Dragging* was selected by Archibald MacLeish for BOA Edition's *New Poets of America Series. For the Kingdom* was published by BOA in 1995.

JAROLD RAMSEY

former Professor of English at the University of Rochester, has published several volumes of poetry, including *The Space Between Us* (1970), *Love in an Earthquake* (1973) and *Hand-Shadows* (1989). His poems have also appeared in such periodicals as *The Atlantic Monthly, Poetry Northwest, The Nation* and *Shenandoah*. His scholarly publications on the North American Indian include *Coyote Was Going There: Indian Literature of the Oregon Country* (1977) and *Reading the Fire: Essays in the Traditional Indian Literature of America* (1999).

STAN SANVEL RUBIN

is Director of the Writers Forum and Videotape Library of the State University of New York College at Brockport, where he also teaches film and creative writing. He is the author of two collections of poetry, *Lost* (1981) and *Midnight* (1985). His poetry has appeared in *The Georgia Review, The Ohio Review, The Kenyon Review, Virginia Quarterly Review, Chelsea*, and other journals. He is co-editor of *The Post Confessionals: Conversations with American Poets of the Eighties*.

JOANNA SCOTT

the Roswell Smith Burrows Professor of English at the University of Rochester, is author of five novels, including *Make Believe*, published in 2000. Her 1990 novel *Arrogance*, based on the life of Austrian painter Egon Schiele, was a finalist for the PEN/Faulkner Award, as was her collection of short fiction, *Various Antidotes* (1994). *The Manikin* (1996) was a finalist for the 1997 Pulitzer Prize. Selected as a MacArthur Fellow in 1993, she has been the recipient of the Pushcart Prize, the Aga Kahn Award, the Rosenthal Award from the Academy and Institute of Arts and Letters and, in 1999, the Lannan Literary Award.

DEBORAH TALL

is the author of four books of poems, most recently *Summons*, which was chosen for the Kathryn A. Morton Poetry Prize by Charles Simic. She has written two books of nonfiction, *The Island of the White Cow: Memories of an Irish Island* and *From Where We Stand: Recovering a Sense of Place*. Tall edits the poetry journal *Seneca Review* and is co-editor of the anthology *The Poet's Notebook*. She teaches writing and literature at Hobart and William Smith Colleges.

LEWIS TURCO

founded and for twenty-seven years directed the Program in Writing Arts at the State University of New York at Oswego. His most recent books are *A Book of Fears*, winner of the first Bordighera Bi-lingual Poetry Prize; *Shaking the Family Tree: A Remembrance*, both published by Bordighera in 1998; *The Book of Literary Terms* (1999) and its companion volume *The Book of Forms*, 3rd edition (2000), both published by the University Press of New England.

KATHLEEN WAKEFIELD

teaches poetry and writing at Writers & Books in Rochester, New York, and in schools in the Rochester area. She is author of a chapbook of poetry, *There and Back*. Her first book of poetry, *Notations on the Visible World*, won the 1999 Anhinga Prize. Her poems have also appeared in *Poetry, The Georgia Review, The Seneca Review* and *The Kenyon Review*. She is the recipient of grants from the New York Foundation of the Arts, the Alumnae Association of Mount Holyoke College and the Constance Saltonstall Foundation for the Arts.

THOM WARD

is Editor/Development Director of BOA Editions, Ltd. and a poet whose work has appeared in many journals, anthologies and newspapers, including *The Christian Science Monitor, The Atlantic Monthly* and *Poetry Northwest*. His first volume of poetry, *Small Boat with Oars of Different Size* (1999), was followed by the chapbook *Tumblekid* (2000). He lives with his wife, three children, two dogs, one cat and a fish in Palmyra, New York.

DAVID WEISS

has published two books of poems, *The Fourth Part of the World,* which won the George Ellison Prize, and *A Pail of Steam*. His novel, *The Mensch,* came out in 1998. He co-edited *The Poet's Notebook*. He teaches at Hobart and William Smith Colleges in Geneva, New York.

ANONYMOUS

(Saint Elizabeth), a Franconian work dated "just before 1500 A.D.," represents Princess Elizabeth of Hungary who was sainted for her works of compassion and charity. The jug of wine and loaf of bread symbolize her charity.

MILTON AVERY

(1883-1965) was an American figurative painter whose simplification of form and composition reflected his keen interest in Henri Matisse. Recent studies have also indicated influence from the nineteenth-century French artist Puvis de Chavannes, in particular that artist's *Girls by the Seashore* at the Louvre.

JAMES HENRY BEARD

(1812-1893) was born in Buffalo, New York, and moved to Painesville, Ohio, with his family in 1823. Essentially self-taught, Beard became an itinerant artist before settling, in 1835, in Cincinnati where he painted genre scenes, portraits (including those of John Quincy Adams and Henry Clay) and chairs. Beard served in the Union Army and after the war settled permanently in New York City. *The Night Before the Battle* is a rare allegorical narrative of the Civil War and apparently refers to the Richmond campaign of early April,1865, "the beginning of the end of the Confederate States of America."

ALBERT BIERSTADT

(1830-1902) was born in Germany and became one of the members of the so-called Rocky Mountain School of artists who painted the natural wonders of the American West. *The Sierras Near Lake Tahoe* was painted during the artist's second trip to the West. His companion on this trip, Fitz Hugh Ludlow, later recounted arriving at Lake Tahoe: "Here, virtually at the end of our overland journey, since our feet pressed the green borders of the Golden State, we sat to rest, feeling that one short hour translated us out of the infernal world into heaven."

RALPH ALBERT BLAKELOCK

(1849-1919) is considered, along with Albert Pinkham Ryder, one of the visionary and mystical painters of the nineteenth century. *Landscape with Trees* is characteristic of Blakelock's style: trees silhouetted against a luminous sky, the use of thick impasto and a nocturnal scene illuminated by moonlight. Blakelock scholar Norman Geske has placed this work in Category One of the Nebraska Blakelock Inventory; according to Geske it is "among the elite of examples which can be regarded as authentic."

CHARLES EPHRAIM BURCHFIELD

(1893-1967) was born in Ashtabula, Ohio. He first studied art at the Cleveland School of Art and, later, at the National Academy in New York City. He moved to Buffalo in 1921 where, a year later, he painted *Springtime in the Pool*. The watercolor well represents Burchfield's personal approach to landscape painting.

GEORGE CATLIN

(1796-1872), a self-taught artist from Wilkes-Barre, Pennsylvania, was one of the first artists to paint the life and culture of Native Americans. In later years, he traveled to South America where, on his last trip in 1857, he painted *Shooting Flamingoes*, commissioned by the Colt Firearms Company for advertising purposes. He wrote about the flamingos of Argentina, and other adventures, in his 1868 book *Last Rambles Among the Indians of the Rocky Mountains and the Andes.*

THOMAS COLE

(1801-1848) was born in England but is considered by many to be America's first great landscape painter and founding father of the Hudson River School. Cole made his first trip to the western New York in 1839 and was apparently the first professional artist to visit and sketch the area around the town of Geneseo. *Genesee Scenery*, depicting the Deh-go-ya-soh ("Nameless Spirits") Creek in Letchworth State Park is the study for the painting of the same name at the Museum of Art, Rhode Island School of Design. Both were done following Cole's 1847 trip to the area. A pencil sketch of the site is at the Detroit Institute of the Arts.

GUSTAVE COURBET

(1819-1877) is considered "the father of modern realism." The commonplace subject matter of his 1849 painting *The Stonebreakers* shocked the Parisian art world when it was exhibited at the Salon of 1850. The Gallery's painting shows Courbet returning to the theme over thirty years later. The revolutionary *Stonebreakers* of 1849 was lost in the 1945 firebombing of Dresden.

RALSTON CRAWFORD

(1906-1978) was an early American modernist who was part of the Precisionist movement. Drawing its subject matter from the industrial world, their work is characterized by a hard-edged, geometric simplification of form. *Whitestone Bridge* connects New York City with Long Island.

ROY DE FOREST
(b. 1930), though born in Nebraska, is associated with the San Francisco Bay area where he has lived since studying at the California School of Fine Arts. A mix of "high" and "low" styles of art, De Forest's work has been described as "a sort of Marx Brothers fauve" and "a California version of the Peaceable Kingdom."

EDWIN DICKINSON
(1891-1978) was a figurative painter often referred to as a "Romantic Realist." Dickinson and his family spent the winter of 1937-38 in the south of France. He painted *Snow on Quai, Sanary* on January 5, 1938, from inside a balcony window at the Hotel Beau Port in the port of Sanary on the Mediterranean. An inscription at the lower right reads "1st snow in 10 yrs," referring to the unusual weather conditions at the time.

ASHER BROWN DURAND
(1796-1886) was one of the leading artists of the Hudson River School. In the summer of 1859, he visited western New York where he painted seven oil studies of the Geneseo area. One of the studies, *Oaks at Geneseo*, is considered the source for the Gallery's 1860 studio painting *Genesee Oaks*. The painting depicts the area of the Big Tree Treaty where, in 1797, the Seneca (represented by Red Jacket) sold four million acres of Iroquois land for $100,000.

BERNARD DUVIVIER
(1762-1837) was born in Flanders. He received his initial art training in Brugues before moving to Paris where he assimilated the neoclassical style of Jacques-Louis David. *Cleopatra Captured by Roman Soldiers after the Death of Mark Antony* is a scene taken directly from Plutarch's *Life of Mark Antony* where Cleopatra is restrained from committing suicide by a Roman soldier. Like the literary source, the pose of Cleopatra was also taken from classical antiquity, specifically the *Laocoon.*

THOMAS EAKINS
(1844-1916) is considered one of the masters of American painting. A native of Philadelphia, he studied in Europe and later taught at the Pennsylvania Academy of the Fine Arts. *William H. Macdowell*, a portrait of his father-in-law, is an example of the artist's "uncompromising realism." Eakins painted Macdowell seven times in addition to making watercolor studies and photographs of the sitter.

JANE FREILICHER
(b. 1924) is one of America's foremost contemporary landscape painters. Mecox Bay is located at the eastern end of Long Island near the artist's summer residence. *View Over Mecox* combines two major motifs: interior studio space and the Long Island landscape.

RICHARD LA BARRE GOODWIN
(1840-1910) was born in Albany, New York, and lived for a time in Rochester. His father was a painter and, presumably, his first teacher. He made his living from portraiture but preferred to paint landscape and still-life scenes.

DOUGLAS WARNER GORSLINE
(1913-1985) was born in Rochester, New York, and, as a child, studied life drawing at the Creative Workshop at the Memorial Art Gallery. He later studied at the Mechanic's Institute (now Rochester Institute of Technology) and at the Yale School of Fine Art before enrolling in classes at the Art Students League in New York. At the League, he met Elizabeth "Zippy" Perkins, his future wife and the model in *Bar Scene*. She was the daughter of Maxwell Perkins, the noted editor of *Scribners*.

NANCY S. GRAVES
(1940-1996) was born in western Massachusetts and studied at Vassar College and Yale University. Her work often reflects her absorption of the lessons of modernism (especially Matisse and the Abstract Expressionists), as well as her deep interest in the sciences, such as anthropology, paleontology and oceanography.

MARTIN JOHNSON HEADE
(1819-1904) found his central motif in the anonymous salt marshes near Newburyport, Massachusetts. *Newbury Hayfield at Sunset*, painted the year of Heade's first visit to Newburyport, is one of the earliest examples in his oeuvre.

JAN DAVIDSZ. DE HEEM
(1606-1684) was one of the most influential masters of seventeenth-century Dutch still-life painting. He spent most of his career in Antwerp where his works were collected by both nobility and wealthy merchants. It is felt that he painted his self-portrait in a reflection of the roemer's cup while seated at his easel in front of the studio window.

WINSLOW HOMER

(1836-1910) first appeared on the American art scene with his graphic and telling narratives of the Civil War. He seriously turned to painting after the war and soon created some of the iconic works in American art, from Adirondack landscapes to Gloucester genre scenes. The last decades of his life were spent at Prout's Neck, Maine, where he painted many of his great seascapes. *The Artist's Studio in an Afternoon Fog* depicts his home and studio at Prout's Neck. He painted his watercolor, *Paddling at Dusk*, during the summer of 1892 at Mink Pond in the Adirondacks. The figure in the boat is Homer's good friend (and fellow North Woods Club member) J. Ernest Yalden.

JOHN FREDERICK KENSETT

(1816-1872) was a member of the Hudson River School whose carefully delineated forms and surface textures, as well as interest in light and atmospheric conditions, are evident in his *A Showery Day, Lake George*. Kensett visited this popular Adirondack resort (a favorite site for artists of the Hudson River School) during the summer of 1853 and painted the view looking northward toward the Narrows and the Black Mountain and Tongue Mountain ranges. The Gallery's painting is similar to Kensett's painting *Lake George* (1869) at the Metropolitan Museum of Art.

PAUL KLEE

(1879-1940), considered one of the masters of modernism, was born in Switzerland and trained in Germany where he was affiliated with the Bauhaus. *Fairy Tales* well represents the artist's highly imaginative, at times whimsical, world of fantasy.

JOHN KOCH

(1909-1978) was a self-taught artist who came to be known as the "modern Vermeer." One of his major themes was the relationship between artist and model. *Interlude* depicts the moments of relaxation and contemplation between formal poses. The interior is of Koch's home on Central Park West in New York City.

JACOB LAWRENCE

(1917-2000) was born in Atlantic City but spent most of his early years in New York City. He first studied art in an after-school arts and crafts program at the 135th Street branch of the public library. His narrative panels depicting African American history established him as one of the major figures in late twentieth-century American art.

KATHLEEN CUNNINGHAM MCENERY

(1885-1971) was born in Brooklyn and studied at the Pratt Institute of Art and later with Robert Henri at the New York School of Art. *Woman in an Ermine Collar* reflects Henri's dark palette and summary brushwork and seems related to his *Young Woman in Black* (1902) at the Art Institute of Chicago. McEnery moved to Rochester in 1914 after marrying Francis E. Cunningham. She was head of the Gallery's Art Committee from 1945-1971 and an Honorary Life Member of the Gallery's Board of Managers beginning in 1927.

CLAUDE MONET

(1840-1926), one of the masters of French Impressionism, painted *Waterloo Bridge, Veiled Sun* during his third and final visit to London in 1901. He stayed at the Savoy Hotel on the Embankment and painted various views of the Thames, including a series of Waterloo Bridge.

WALTER MURCH

(1907-1967) was born in Canada where he began his study of art. Later, he studied with realist Kenneth Hayes Miller at the Art Students League in New York and, concurrently, with modernist Ashile Gorky at the Grand Central School of Art.

BEVERLY PEPPER

(b. 1924) was born in Brooklyn, New York. She first studied commercial design at Pratt Institute. Later, she studied at the Art Students League and Brooklyn College before traveling to Paris where she studied with, among others, Fernand Léger. Happily for the theme of this book, she is also the mother of noted poet Jorie Graham.

FAIRFIELD PORTER

(1907-1975) was an art critic and author, a painter and a poet. He remains one of the preeminent landscape painters of the twentieth century. *The Beginnings of the Field* is a scene of Southampton, Long Island, where the artist lived from 1949 on.

RACHEL RUYSCH

(1664-1750), one of the first women whose paintings gained international recognition, was court painter to the elector palatine in Düsseldorf. *Floral Still Life* is based, in part, on a painting by the seventeenth-century German artist Abraham Mignon who was a student of Jan Davidsz. de Heem (p.106).

EVERETT SHINN

(1876-1953) was one of members of the so-called Ashcan School, a group of realist artists who painted the miscellany of New York City life during the first decades of the twentieth century. Sullivan Street, the locale of the Gallery's painting, is south of Washington Square in Greenwich Village.

WAYNE THIEBAUD

(b. 1920) is one of the founding members of the California contingent of Pop artists. Though best known for his highly colored, painterly canvases of baked goods, Thiebaud is also known for his cityscapes and landscapes, many of which date back to the 1960s. A 1971 lithograph, *Silver Landscape*, and a 1970 pencil drawing, *River Pond Study*, both in the Gallery's collection, relate to the painting *River Pond.*

JOHN HENRY TWACHTMAN

(1853-1902), one of America's leading Impressionists, was trained in Munich and Paris before settling in Greenwich, Connecticut, in the late 1880s. Twachtman built a white lattice bridge on his Connecticut property which became a favorite motif. *The White Bridge* is one of several known versions (others are at the Art Institute of Chicago, the Minneapolis Institute of Art and the Georgia Museum of Fine Arts, University of Georgia).

FRANCESCO UBERTINI (*called Il Bacchiacca*)

(1494-1557) was born near Florence, studied with Perugino and served as a court painter to Cosimo de Medici in Florence for nearly two decades. Scholars have noted the specific influence of Dürer (*Life of the Virgin* series), Michelangelo (*Battle of Cascina* cartoon) and others in *The Conversion of Saint Paul.* The bearded figure to the left of Paul is said to be the artist's self-portrait.

LEONARD WELLS VOLK

(1828-1895) was raised in western New York and may have lived in Rochester for a period of time. He began his sculpture career in St.Louis and, after traveling in Europe, settled in Chicago in 1857. In April of 1860, Lincoln sat for his life mask while in Chicago. The following month, Lincoln was nominated for the presidency and Volk traveled to Springfield, Illinois, to make casts of his hands for use (along with the face) in full-size sculpture, including Volk's 1892 Lincoln monument in Rochester.

EDOUARD VUILLARD

(1868-1940) was a member of the Nabis, a group of late nineteenth-century French artists who preferred small, intimate subject matter while formally concentrating on flat areas of color and rich pattern. Aurelien Marie Lugné-Poë, a long-time friend of Vuillard, was an actor, director and avant-garde theatrical producer for the Théatre de l'Oeuvre.

Checklist

ANONYMOUS
(German, ca. 1500)
St. Elizabeth with Jug of Wine and Loaf of Bread,
ca. 1500
Wood, 30 in.
Bequest of Elizabeth Stebbins in
memory of her mother, Elizabeth Sibley. 57.7

AVERY, MILTON
(American, 1893-1965)
Haircut by the Sea, 1943
Oil on canvas; 44 in. x 32 in.
Gift of Roy R. Neuberger. 63.21

BEARD, JAMES HENRY
(American, 1814-1893)
The Night Before the Battle, 1865
Oil on canvas; 30 1/2 in. x 44 1/2 in.
Gift of Dr. Ronald M. Lawrence. 78.15

BIERSTADT, ALBERT
(American, 1830-1902)
The Sierras Near Lake Tahoe, California, 1865
Oil on panel; 14 15/16 in. x 21 1/16 in.
Clara and Edwin Strasenburgh Fund
and Marion Stratton Gould Fund. 92.78

BLAKELOCK, RALPH ALBERT
(American, 1847-1919)
Landscape with Trees, ca. 1880
Oil on canvas; 8 in. x 12 1/4 in.
Anonymous gift. 94.34

BURCHFIELD, CHARLES EPHRAIM
(American, 1893-1967)
Springtime in the Pool, 1922
Watercolor and gouache on paper;
21 1/8 in. x 18 5/8 in.
Gift of Mrs. Charles H. Babcock. 45.68

CATLIN, GEORGE
(American, 1796-1872)
Shooting Flamingoes, 1857
Oil on canvas; 19 in. x 26 1/2 in.
R. T. Miller Fund, 1941, transferred to
Marion Stratton Gould Fund, 1949. 41.25

COLE, THOMAS
(American, 1801-1848)
Genesee Scenery, 1846-1847
Oil on panel; 6 1/4 in. x 4 3/8 in.
Gift of Howard and Florence Merritt. 94.40

COURBET, GUSTAVE
(French, 1819-1877)
The Stonebreaker, ca. 1872
Oil on canvas; 17 1/2 in. x 21 1/2 in.
Marion Stratton Gould Fund. 43.11

CRAWFORD, RALSTON
(American, 1906-1978)
Whitestone Bridge, 1939
Oil on canvas; 40 1/4 in. x 32 in.
Marion Stratton Gould Fund. 51.2

DE FOREST, ROY
(American, 1930-)
The Dipolar Girls Take a Voyage on the St. Lawrence, 1970
Acrylic, polymer and charcoal on canvas;
70 3/4 in. x 64 1/2 in.
Gift of Charles and Setta Odoroff in honor of
Maurice and Minnie Odoroff. 86.134

DICKINSON, EDWIN
(American, 1891-1978)
Snow on Quai, Sanary, 1938
Oil on canvas; 21 in. x 18 in.
Gift of Nancy Turner in memory of Richard Turner.
87.62

DURAND, ASHER BROWN
(American, 1796-1886)
Genesee Oaks, 1860
Oil on canvas; 28 1/4 in. x 42 in.
Gift of the Women's Council in honor of
Harris K. Prior. 74.5

DUVIVIER, BERNARD
(French, 1762-1837)
Cleopatra Captured by Roman Soldiers, 1789
Oil on canvas;
45 in. x 58 in. (114.3 cm x 147.32 cm)
Marion Stratton Gould Fund. 84.40

EAKINS, THOMAS
(American, 1844-1916)
William H. Macdowell, ca. 1904
Oil on canvas; 24 in. x 20 in.
Marion Stratton Gould Fund. 41.26

FREILICHER, JANE
(American, 1924-)
View Over Mecox (Yellow Wall), 1991-1993
Oil on linen; 80 in. x 70 in.
Gift of Lynne Lovejoy in memory of her husband,
Dr. Frank Lovejoy, Jr. 99.1

GOODWIN, RICHARD LABARRE
(American, 1840-1910)
A Brace of Ducks, 1885
Oil on canvas; 30 in. x 25 in.
Marion Stratton Gould Fund. 64.39

GORSLINE, DOUGLAS WARNER
(American, 1913-1985)
Bar Scene, 1942
Oil on canvas; 29 1/2 in. x 25 1/4 in.
Purchased through the Art Patrons' Fund.
42.19

GRAVES, NANCY S.
(American, 1940-1995)
Fragment, 1977
Oil and crayon on canvas; 64 in. x 76 in.
Gift of Sharon and Neil Norry;
and Marion Stratton Gould Fund. 85.27

HEEM, JAN DAVIDSZ. DE
(Dutch, 1606-1693)
Still Life
Oil on panel; 14 1/2 in. x 18 in.
Marion Stratton Gould Fund. 49.63

HOMER, WINSLOW
(American, 1836-1910)
Paddling at Dusk, 1892
Watercolor with graphite on wove paper;
15 1/8 in. x 21 7/16 in.
Gift of Dr. and Mrs. James H. Lockhart, Jr. 84.51

HOMER, WINSLOW
(American, 1836-1910)
The Artist's Studio in an Afternoon Fog, 1894
Oil on canvas; 24 in. x 30 1/4 in.
R. T. Miller Fund. 41.32

KENSETT, JOHN FREDERICK
(American, 1816-1872)
A Showery Day, Lake George, ca. 1860
Oil on canvas; 14 1/8 in. x 24 1/8 in.
Marion Stratton Gould Fund. 74.29

KLEE, PAUL
(Swiss, 1879-1940)
Fairy Tales, ca. 1920
Watercolor and gouache on paper; 8 3/16 in. x 10 1/4 in.
Marion Stratton Gould Fund. 57.37

KOCH, JOHN
(American, 1909-1978)
Interlude, 1963
Oil on canvas; 50 1/8 in. x 39 7/8 in.
Gift of Mr. and Mrs. Thomas H. Hawks. 65.12

LAWRENCE, JACOB
(American, 1917-2000)
Summer Street Scene in Harlem, 1948
Tempera on gesso panel; 20 1/16 in. x 24 1/8 in.
Marion Stratton Gould Fund. 91.5

MCENERY, KATHLEEN CUNNINGHAM
(American, 1885-1971)
Woman in an Ermine Collar, 1909
Oil on canvas; 76 7/8 in. x 38 3/8 in.
Gift of Joan Cunningham Williams, Peter Cunningham,
and Michael McEnery Cunningham. 83.13

MONET, CLAUDE
(French, 1840-1926)
Waterloo Bridge, Veiled Sun, 1903
Oil on canvas; 25 1/2 in. x 39 1/4 in.
Gift of the estate of Emily and James Sibley Watson. 53.6

MURCH, WALTER
(American, 1907-1967)
Resting Rock, 1961
Oil on canvas; 35 in. x 30 in.
Marion Stratton Gould Fund. 98.78

PEPPER, BEVERLY
(American, 1924-)
Vertical Ventaglio, ca. 1967-1969
Stainless and carbon steel with automotive paint;
104 5/8 in. x 43 1/2 in. x 86 in.
The Charles Rand Penney Collection
of the Memorial Art Gallery. 78.195

PORTER, FAIRFIELD
(American, 1907-1975)
The Beginning of the Fields, 1973
Oil on canvas; 52 in. x 76 1/8 in.
Marion Stratton Gould Fund. 86.132

RUYSCH, RACHEL
(Dutch, 1664/1665-1750)
Floral Still Life, 1686
Oil on canvas; 45 1/8 in. x 34 3/8 in.
Acquired with contributions made in memory of Brenda
Rowntree by her friends, through the Acquisition Fund
of the Women's Council, and the Marion Stratton
Gould Fund. 82.9

SHINN, EVERETT
(American, 1876-1953)
Sullivan Street, 1905
Oil on canvas; 8 in. x 10 in.
Marion Stratton Gould Fund. 45.45

THIEBAUD, WAYNE
(American, 1920-)
River Pond, 1967-1975
Acrylic on canvas; 74 1/8 in. x 76 1/16 in.
Joseph C. Wilson Memorial Fund. 75.421

TWACHTMAN, JOHN HENRY
(American, 1853-1902)
The White Bridge, ca. 1900
Oil on canvas; 30 1/4 in. x 25 1/8 in.
Gift of Emily Sibley Watson. 16.9

UBERTINI, FRANCESCO
(Italian, 1494?-1557)
The Conversion of St. Paul
Oil on panel; 88 in. x 31 in.
Marion Stratton Gould Fund. 54.2

VOLK, LEONARD WELLS
(American, 1828-1895)
Life Mask and Hands of Abraham Lincoln, 1860
Bronze; 9 3/4 in. x 8 1/8 in. x 5 5/8 in.
Maurice R. and Maxine B. Forman Fund. 98.37.1-.2

VUILLARD, EDOUARD
(French, 1868-1940)
Portrait of Lugné Poë, 1891
Oil on paper mounted on cradled panel;
8 3/4 in. x 10 1/2 in.
Gift of Fletcher Steele. 72.18

Copyrights and Credits

Milton Avery, *Haircut by the Sea*, 1943.
© 2001 Milton Avery Trust/Artists Rights Society (ARS), New York.

Ralston Crawford, *Whitestone Bridge*, 1939.
Reproduced with permission from the Estate of Ralston Crawford.

Roy DeForest, *The Dipolar Girls Take a Voyage on the St. Lawrence*, 1970.
Reproduced with permission from the artist.

Edwin Dickinson, *Snow on Quai, Sanary*, 1938.
Reproduced with permission from Helen Dickinson Baldwin.

Jane Freilicher, *View Over Mecox (Yellow Wall)*, 1991-1993.
Reproduced with permission from the artist.

Douglas Gorsline, *Bar Scene*, 1942.
Reproduced with permission from the Estate of Douglas Gorsline.

Nancy Graves, *Fragment*, 1977.
© Nancy Graves Foundation/Licensed by VAGA, New York, NY.

Paul Klee, *Fairy Tales*, 1920.
© 2001 Artists Rights Society (ARS), New York/VG Bild-Kunst, Bonn.

John Koch, *Interlude*, 1963.
Reproduced with permission from Kraushaar Galleries, Inc.
for the Estate of John Koch.

Jacob Lawrence, *Summer Street Scene in Harlem*, 1948.
© Gwendolyn Knight Lawrence, courtesy of the Jacob and Gwendolyn Lawrence Foundation.

Beverly Pepper, *Vertical Ventaglio*, ca. 1967-1969.
© Beverly Pepper/Licensed by VAGA, New York, NY/ Marlborough Gallery, NY.

Fairfield Porter, *The Beginning of the Fields*, 1973.
Reproduced with permission from the Fiduciary Trust Company for the Estate of Fairfield Porter.

Edouard Vuillard, *Portrait of Lugné Pöe*, 1891.
© 2001 Artists Rights Society (ARS), New York/ADAGP, Paris.

Wayne Thiebaud, *River Pond*, 1967-1975.
© Wayne Thiebaud/Licensed by VAGA, New York, NY.

Copy editor: John Blanpied
Production editor: Deborah Rothman
Project coordinator: Carolyn Wilson
Rights and reproduction coordinator: Susan Nurse
Photographer: James M. Via
Design: Van Auken Margolis & Associates
Color and image assembly: Jim Herschell, Flower City Printing
Printing: Tucker Printers